SAUCES
RECONSIDERED

Rowman & Littlefield Studies in Food and Gastronomy

General Editor: Ken Albala, Professor of History,
University of the Pacific (kalbala@pacific.edu)

Rowman & Littlefield Executive Editor:
Suzanne Staszak-Silva (sstaszak-silva@rowman.com)

Food studies is a vibrant and thriving field encompassing not only cooking and eating habits but also issues such as health, sustainability, food safety, and animal rights. Scholars in disciplines as diverse as history, anthropology, sociology, literature, and the arts focus on food. The mission of **Rowman & Littlefield Studies in Food and Gastronomy** is to publish the best in food scholarship, harnessing the energy, ideas, and creativity of a wide array of food writers today. This broad line of food-related titles will range from food history, interdisciplinary food studies monographs, general interest series, and popular trade titles to textbooks for students and budding chefs, scholarly cookbooks, and reference works.

Appetites and Aspirations in Vietnam: Food and Drink in the Long Nineteenth Century, by Erica J. Peters
Three World Cuisines: Italian, Mexican, Chinese, by Ken Albala
Food and Social Media: You Are What You Tweet, by Signe Rousseau
Food and the Novel in Nineteenth-Century America, by Mark McWilliams
Man Bites Dog: Hot Dog Culture in America, by Bruce Kraig and Patty Carroll
A Year in Food and Beer: Recipes and Beer Pairings for Every Season, by Emily Baime and Darin Michaels
Celebraciones Mexicanas: History, Traditions, and Recipes, by Andrea Lawson Gray and Adriana Almazán Lahl
The Food Section: Newspaper Women and the Culinary Community, by Kimberly Wilmot Voss
Small Batch: Pickles, Cheese, Chocolate, Spirits, and the Return of Artisanal Foods, by Suzanne Cope
Food History Almanac: Over 1,300 Years of World Culinary History, Culture, and Social Influence, by Janet Clarkson
Cooking and Eating in Renaissance Italy: From Kitchen to Table, by Katherine A. McIver

SAUCES RECONSIDERED

APRÈS ESCOFFIER

Gary Allen

ROWMAN & LITTLEFIELD
Lanham • Boulder • New York • London

Published by Rowman & Littlefield
An imprint of The Rowman & Littlefield Publishing Group, Inc.
4501 Forbes Boulevard, Suite 200, Lanham, Maryland 20706
www.rowman.com

6 Tinworth Street, London SE11 5AL, United Kingdom

British Library Cataloguing in Publication Information Available

Library of Congress Cataloging-in-Publication Data
Names: Allen, Gary (Gary J.), author.
Title: Sauces reconsidered : après Escoffier / Gary Allen.
Description: Lanham, Maryland : the Rowman & Littlefield, [2019] | Series:
  Rowman & Littlefield studies in food and gastronomy | Includes
  bibliographical references and index.
Identifiers: LCCN 2018029461 (print) | LCCN 2018032723 (ebook) | ISBN
  9781538115145 (electronic) | ISBN 9781538115138 (cloth : alk. paper)
Subjects: LCSH: Sauces. | Sauces—History. | Escoffier, A. (Auguste),
  1846-1935. | LCGFT: Cookbooks.
Classification: LCC TX819.A1 (ebook) | LCC TX819.A1 A37 2019 (print) | DDC
  641.81/4—dc23
LC record available at https://lccn.loc.gov/2018029461

♾™ The paper used in this publication meets the minimum requirements
of American National Standard for Information Sciences—Permanence of
Paper for Printed Library Materials, ANSI/NISO Z39.48-1992.

Printed in the United States of America

For my wife, Karen Philipp,
who is saucy in a good way.

CONTENTS

10 **EMULSIONS**   127

11 **CULTURED SAUCES**   139

12 **COMPOSITES**   147

AFTERWORD   169

NOTES   171

REFERENCES   183

INDEX   189

x

ACKNOWLEDGMENTS

It would be unthinkable *not* to thank Harold McGee for doing so much to make the science of the kitchen accessible to cooks. More than anyone else, he stripped away the untested assumptions and accepted "facts" about what we do when we cook—and replaced them with methods that actually work (and explained *why* they work).

Nor can I omit my friend Robert DelGrosso, since this book grew directly from conversations we shared when we both worked at the Hyde Park campus of The Culinary Institute of America (The CIA). Bob is one of those rare individuals who combines scientific outlook and artistic ability with a broad knowledge of the humanities—and manages to bring all that experience into the kitchen.

Speaking of The CIA, the Conrad N. Hilton Library and its wonderful staff have been generous (and patient) with their time and knowledge. I've availed myself of their largesse many times, for most of my books and several of my articles, and I'm immensely appreciative.

Ken Albala—my editor, collaborator, and friend—had faith in this project when it was little more than an idea. He and the rest of the production staff at Rowman & Littlefield, especially Suzanne Staszak-Silva and Patricia Stevenson, have literally made this book what it is. That said, it is only fair to admit that any errors, egregious blunders, and unforgivable oversights encountered herein are entirely my own contributions.

INTRODUCTION

What is a sauce? Everyone knows the answer, right? It's that fluid substance we pour over our food to make it taste better.

Naturally, the real answer is a bit more complicated (or this book could be reduced to just those last fourteen words) and poses some interesting questions. For example, some of those "fluid substances" are by-products of the cooking process that serve to reinforce the flavor of the main ingredient (*jus* and pan gravy are familiar examples), while others are made separately and provide a culinary counterpoint to the primary ingredient. The latter include, among others, the "marinara" that coats a pizza, the hollandaise atop eggs Benedict, and a vast array of condiments, either freshly prepared or commercially made—from mustard, ketchup, and mayonnaise to Worcestershire and *sriracha*.

Then there is the question of viscosity. How much viscosity is too much? When does a sauce cease to be a sauce and become better described as a paste? And what if an ingredient, like Chinese sesame paste—which is more solid than Middle Eastern tahini—is thinned with other, more liquid ingredients to make something that is clearly sauce-like? Does that make it a kind of proto sauce?

Still more issues add complexity to the discussion: How does the intended usage of one of these flavorful liquids affect its position in a hierarchy of sauces? Where do we even *place* the sauce relative to other foodstuffs? Do we pool it under, pour it over, mix it thoroughly throughout, serve it on the side (in condiment bottles or little bowls of dipping liquid), or even encapsulate it inside (like the agar-covered pearls of molecular gastronomy or Shanghai-style soup dumplings)?

So, we've already begun to probe the variables that delineate possible categories for sauces—the rude beginnings of a kind of taxonomy. Many of our decisions will place individual sauces somewhere on a continuous spectrum of sauces, rarely all one form or another. Attempting to force an ingredient into one of two categories (sauce or nonsauce) is almost as useless as separating the entire animal kingdom into male and female. While that does provide one kind of distinction, it tells us very little about individual species and how they relate to one another. Nature, including the nature of sauces, is not so easily crammed into one cubbyhole or another.

Needless to say, we are not the first to have tried to make sense of the world of sauces—some have had more success than others. There is nothing completely new under the sun. This book attempts to build on previous efforts and, possibly, to create a more universal taxonomy of sauces. If, like Isaac Newton, we are to see farther by standing on the shoulders of giants—a notion he borrowed from a series of giants that goes all the way back to the Roman poet Lucan—then we must begin with the sauces and the sauce classifications of the past. It remains to be seen whether—after visiting Westminster Abbey and literally standing on the shoulders (and the rest of what remains) of Isaac Newton—our view has been much enhanced by the experience.

Note: When possible, historical recipes have been formatted as modern recipes. However, some could not be so arranged without fundamentally altering their "flavor." Their quaint style is a part of that "flavor" that we discard at our peril. Likewise, the unusual spellings in these recipes have been left as found and uncorrected. Think of them as spicy ingredients that have somehow gone out of fashion after decades or centuries of neglect.

A FEW WORDS
ABOUT SALT

It's almost impossible to discuss sauces without mentioning sodium chloride (NaCl). Salt is so important that the very words "sauce" and "salsa" (not to mention "sausage," "salary," and "salubrious") are derived, ultimately, from the Latin *sal*, meaning "salt." It is so basic that *The Deipnosophistae* of Athenaeus quotes the Cynic Antiphanes as saying, "Of the relishes which come from the sea we always have one, and that day in, day out. I mean salt."[1]

It's not a coincidence that Matthew 5:13–16 has Jesus saying, "Ye are the salt of the earth: but if the salt have lost his savour, wherewith shall it be salted? It is thenceforth good for nothing, but to be cast out, and to be trodden under foot of men." We are nothing if we're not "worth our salt"—and neither are our sauces.

This is not just a Western concept. According to Zhou Hongcheng, the ancient Chinese had a saying: "Oh salt, he is a General in the Chinese cuisine."

This saying, used earlier but recorded by Ban Gu during the Eastern Han Dynasty (25–220 CE), shows the importance of salt in all sauces.

Salt crystals bring cultural meanings and give people food choices in sauce manufacture. Salt supplements enhance each sauce, and Chinese food preparation reflects people's affection for sauce and salt in their lives. In China, people do not get their salt from a salt shaker. They get theirs using many different sauces as they prepare their dishes. Thus, in China, salt and sauce are great partners.[2]

Salt is essential to life for all of us (animals travel miles just for a chance to lick soil containing even a trace of salt). However, for anyone afflicted by hypertension, too much salt can be dangerous. Fortunately, excess salt is eliminated by the kidneys of healthy people, so—for them, at least—warnings about NaCl's dangers should be taken with a grain of you-know-what.

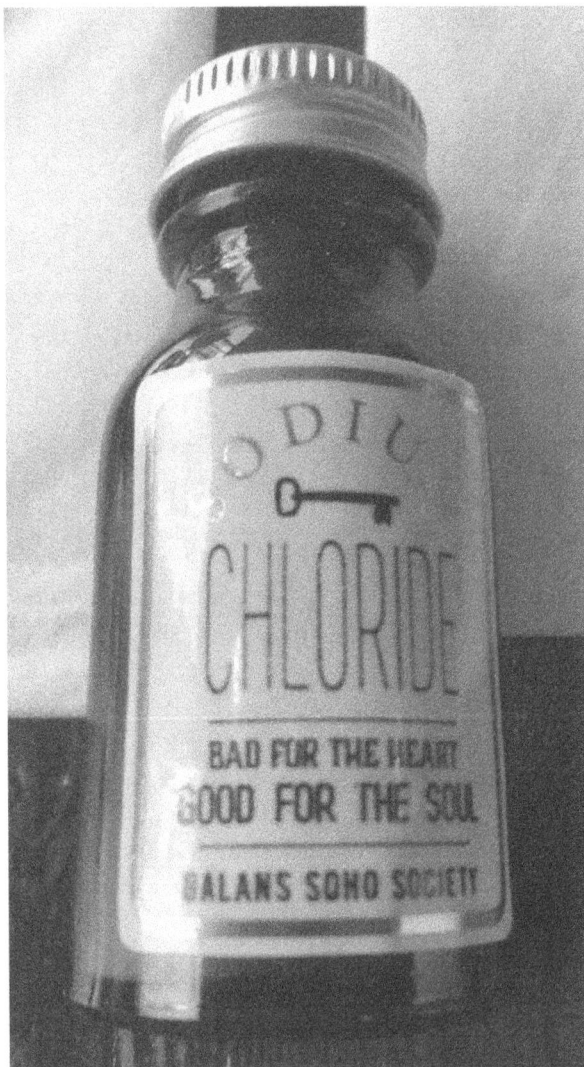

Salt, as served by folks who care more about taste than medical proscriptions. *Source:* Gary Allen

I

ANCIENS REGIMES

1

SO MANY RICH SAUCES

Many food histories open their discussion of early sauces by referring, like Isaac Newton's famous quote, to the Romans. This seems reasonable because much of what we've learned about the history of cooking has been gleaned from cookbooks—and the earliest known cookbook is *De re coquinaria*. It was attributed to Apicius and compiled in the fourth century CE, but it was not actually written by that famous first-century gourmet. It was assembled from various sources and merely named for Apicius. Think of it as old-school (very old-school) celebrity marketing.

It's always difficult to determine when a recipe was first created. Recipes don't usually appear in written form until well after they've proven successful enough for people to want to save them for others to prepare. Also, "new" recipes are often variations on older recipes, so who's to say when they were really created? We can safely assume that the recipes in *De re coquinaria* were already "classic" by the time someone decided to collect them together in book form.

About a century before *De re coquinaria* was compiled, Athenaeus wrote *The Deipnosophistae*, a detailed account of luxurious dining in the period. It was not a cookbook, but he described many dishes—and mentioned the sauces that accompanied them. Athenaeus collected his "recipes" from a number of books—many from ancient Greece—that have not survived to our time, so his accounts provide a way to peer a little further back in time than would otherwise be possible.

His book describes a simple sauce from *The Slave-Teacher* (by Phere-crates, a comic playwright, who lived about the same time as Aristophanes). Pherecrates wrote some eighteen plays, but the few fragments that survive do so largely because of Athenaeus.

> Tell us how the dinner is progressing. Well then, you are to have a piece of eel, a squid, some lamb, a slice of sausage, a boiled foot, a liver, a rib, a vast number of birds, cheese with honey sauce, and a portion of beef.[1]

Sauce-related fragments of several plays by Sopater of Paphos appear in *The Deipnosophistae*.[2] For example, in his *Hippolytus*, he wrote, "How the fecund miscarried matrix rounds out cheese-like in the stew, covered with white sauce!"[3] A "matrix" was the uterus of a pig (apparently a "nose-to-tail" delicacy in the ancient world). His *Physiologus* mentions "a well boil'd slice of paunch of pig holding within a sharp and biting gravy." "Pig's paunch" is what we call pork belly, or uncured bacon. The Greeks, like us, cut the fattiness of such rich meats with tangy sauces. In the *Silphæ*, Sopater says, "You may eat a slice of boil'd pig's paunch, Dipping it in a bitter sauce of rue."[4] In *Amphictyons*, Teleclides dreamed that

Fish too came straight unto men's doors,
And fried themselves all ready,
Dished themselves up, and stood before
The guests upon the tables.
A stream of soup did flow along
In front of all the couches,
Rolling down lumps of smoking meat;
And rivulets of white sauce
. . . There too were cutlets of broiled fish well seasoned
With sauce of every kind, and cook, and country.
. . . And streams of sauce which flow
Straight down from Plutus' own springs,
For all the guests to relish.[5]

This sounds like the medieval *pays de cocaigne* or the hobo utopian song "Big Rock Candy Mountain" by Haywire Mac (Harry McClintock).

We often hear of the Roman fish sauces *garum* and *liquamen* (we'll discuss them at greater length further along), and it is clear from reading Athenaeus that such fermented sauces were common in Greek cooking.

Amphis notes that the oil produced in Thurii is particularly good: the oil in Thurii, lentil soup in Gela. Fermented fish-sauce.

Cratinus: Your basket will be full of fish-sauce.

Pherecrates: He got his beard dirty with the fish-sauce.

Sophocles in Triptolemus: . . . of sauce made of preserved fish.

Plato: They're going to choke me to death by dipping me in rotten fish-sauce.[6]

However, the use of fish sauces is even older, perhaps a thousand years older. Reading through Babylonian cuneiform tablets,[7] we encounter many references to *siqqu*, which is the Mesopotamian equivalent of *garum*. *Siqqu* was fermented protein (from fish, shellfish, or even grasshoppers) in concentrated brine.

Most of the surviving recipes from Mesopotamia are for meats cooked in complex, highly seasoned broths. These rich broths (usually described, lovingly, as "fatty") were sometimes served with the boiled meats or separately, like a soup. Blood or crumbs of *bappiru* (bread that was both a by-product and an ingredient of the beer-making process) thickened the broth, a technique that survived into the Middle Ages and beyond. Indeed, *pearà* (a rich sauce made from a complicated stock and bread-crumbs cooked in beef marrow and heavily seasoned with black pepper) is still the cornerstone of Veronese *bollito misto*. The recipe is rumored to date to the ninth century, which corresponds with the beginnings of the Venetian spice trade, so all that expensive pepper was appropriately—and conspicuously—extravagant.

Here is a typical Mesopotamian recipe (note the absence of many of the details—method, amounts, temperature, and timing—we expect in a recipe):

Historic Recipe: Dodder Broth

Not fresh meat but rather "salted" meat is used. Prepare water; add fat; . . . some crushed dodder; onion, samidu, coriander; cumin; leek and garlic. . . . With the pot resting on the heat, the broth is ready to serve.[8]

"Dodder" is Jean Bottéro's translation of *kasû*. He suspected that it might have been an invasive weed of the *Cuscuta* genus.[9] Laura Kelley says it's much more likely to be "wild licorice (*Glycyrrhiza glabra*), and . . . was used by the Mesopotamians both in cooking and in making beer,"[10] which sounds much tastier.

Bottéro didn't know what *samidu* was either, but he thought that its context in other recipes suggested that it was a precious spice of some kind. Kelley notes, "Looking to modern languages, however, I found that in Hebrew and Syrian, *semida* means 'fine meal' and, in Greek, *semidalis* is used to denote 'the finest flour.' According to the University of Chicago's Assyrian Dictionary, *semidu* is also defined as semolina."[11]

The use of flour or breadcrumbs as a sauce thickener is obviously ancient, but it is certainly not obsolete. British bread sauce is a survivor from medieval kitchens (stew stale breadcrumbs in milk with butter and onions, and then season with a mixture of spices that would seem familiar to any thirteenth-century cook: bay leaves, cloves, mace, and pepper). In the same fashion, the *rouille* of Provence is a paste made by pounding breadcrumbs, chiles, garlic, and saffron in olive oil. It's added to each diner's portion of *bouillabaisse* to taste.

When we read the satirists (such as Petronius and Juvenal), we encounter an exaggerated version of what the Romans ate, but their accounts had to be close enough to reality to be immediately recognizable to their audiences. For example, when—during the famous feast of Trimalchio (in *The Satyricon*)—the fish course arrives, we're told, "At the corners of the tray stood four little gravy boats, all shaped like the satyr Marsyas, with phalluses from spouts and a spicy hot gravy dripping down over several large fish swimming about in the lagoon of the tray."[12] The excess might be laughable, but the fact that sauces were served was expected. "Gravy" is an unfortunate choice of words in the translation, since we have a strong culturally identified notion of "gravy" that would not have made sense to a diner in ancient Rome. Trimalchio's "spicy hot gravy" is nothing like our gravy (meat juices thickened with flour); rather, it is *garum piperatum*—a heavily peppered Roman fish sauce.

In his fourteenth satire, Juvenal lampoons the Roman taste for crude excess, such as when a sauce overwhelms a delicacy:

Who, with a gourmand sire, a hoary old glutton as teacher,
Knows all about peeling truffles, all about seasoning mushrooms,
All about drowning in gravy the delicate beccaficoes.[13]

"Beccaficoes" are our ortolans—tiny endangered birds that cause wealthy
gourmets to become culinary outlaws. Even today, we laugh at the culinary
excess of gourmets sitting at table with napkins over their heads to prevent
the escape of any trace of ortolan vapor (or, perhaps, to hide the shame of
indulging in their illicit gastronomic bliss).

While the satirists provide small glimpses of Roman sauce consumption,
De re coquinaria gives us a better idea of its extent. The text is divided into
books, each devoted to a single category: "Mise en Place," "Meat Dishes,"
"Greens," "Compound Dishes," "Pulses," "Fowl," "Luxury Dishes,"
"Quadrupeds," "Seafood," and "Fish."

One book in *De re coquinaria*, "Epimeles" (meaning essentially *mise en
place*, a French term that refers to the sorts of things a cook would do in
advance, preparations any kitchen would keep on hand), lists only a few
basic sauces:

A couple of cumin sauces (one specifically for oysters and shellfish),
containing pepper, lovage, dried mint, malabathrum (foliage of the
cinnamon plant), plenty of cumin, honey, vinegar, and *liquamen*

Two *laser* sauces (*laser* was a synonym for *silphium*, an odoriferous asa-
foetida-like resin) flavored with honey, vinegar, and *liquamen*, as well
as various combinations of herbs (parsley, mint, spikenard, lovage,
dill, rue) and the usual malabathrum and silphium

Mortaria, pesto-like pounded fresh herbs (mint, rue, cilantro, and fennel), plus honey, *liquamen*, lovage, and pepper, made sweet and sour
with vinegar

A pair of sauces based on *oenogarum* (mixtures of wine and *liquamen*),
with coriander, honey, lovage, pepper, rue, and oil, or with honey,
lovage, pepper, savory, thyme, and oil

Oxygarum, an aid to digestion made with cardamom, cumin, mint, and
pepper, sweetened with honey and thinned with *liquamen* and vinegar

Oxyporium, a honey-based sauce consisting of cumin, ginger, dates, pepper, and rue

With the fall of Rome, cookbooks as sources of information about sauces pretty much disappeared. I'm sure that sauces were still served in the so-called Dark Ages, but we really started hearing about them only after medieval kitchens started showing the influence of Crusaders' experiences of the spice-based cookery of the Holy Lands (and even more so after the late fifteenth century, when printing made the wide-scale publishing of cookbooks possible).

While European kitchens left few traces during those dark years, Islam was highly literate and not only had the kind of rich court life that encouraged the development of haute cuisine but also documented it in writing.

Like the Romans and the Mesopotamians before them, Islamic cooks relied heavily on salty fermented sauces to add umami (the so-called fifth taste, roughly like our savory) to their dishes. Their equivalent of *garum* and *siqqu* was called *murri*,[14] and it came in two different versions: the familiar fish sauce and a paste-like ingredient made from fermented barley bread. Both were dark and savory—very much like Chinese soy sauce in character and function. Another sauce was made from spiced grape juice, a thick syrup reduced to the consistency of molasses.

Unlike the Romans, Islamic cooks had access to sugar, with which they prepared countless syrups that they used either directly or in combination with fruits, spices, and *murri*. Their religion forbade the use of wine, of course, but they were allowed *nabîdh raihâni* (a weak basil-scented brew). Islamic cooks thickened their sauces with ground almonds and walnuts in addition to dried fruits (such as raisins and dates).

While Roman cooks liked to incorporate bitter tastes, like rue, Islamic cooks relied on sweet spices: cinnamon, cloves, ginger, and nutmeg. They were early masters of maceration and distillation, so many of their dishes were perfumed with rose water, orange-blossom water, and infusions of violets and lavender.

Arabic flavors and techniques came to dominate European court cookery well into the Renaissance. Only with *The Opera* of Bartolomeo Scappi (1570) do we see the beginning of the end of medieval sauce cookery in Italy. Ginger and cinnamon were less used, but sauces based on fruits (apples, cherries, gooseberries, mulberries, pomegranates, prunes, quince, raisins, and red currants), nuts (almonds and walnuts), and various forms of *agrodolce* (bittersweet, based on citrus—such as bitter orange—and/or verjuice, combined with honey or sugar) still reflect the Arabic influence on European cooking. Scappi was also fond of using rose water in his recipes, another nod to Islamic traditions. He was not only looking to the past; he also had a recipe that foreshadowed today's pesto (it incorporated several herbs [arugula, burnet, mint, parsley, sorrel, and spinach] and nuts [almonds or filberts] but no oil, garlic, or cheese).

As European cookery started moving away from Middle Eastern flavors, their influence survived, long afterward, in an unlikely place. Spanish cooks held on to these traditions longer than their neighbors and, through colonization, influenced the cooking of Mexico. Classic *mole poblano*, with its complex sauce of spices, thickened with almonds and raisins, could easily be mistaken for an Arabic dish. Before the New World was discovered, Islamic cooks wouldn't have had chocolate and chiles (so they never created *mole poblano*) or pumpkin seeds; otherwise, they probably would have invented sauces that resembled Mexican *pipians*.

While attempts to classify sauces really began in earnest in France, the ancient Chinese also tried to categorize sauce cookery.

> The first and earliest are meat sauces. This sauce group include[s] those from four-legged animals and those made from poultry including chicken and goose. There are also meat sauces made from wild beasts and from small animals such as rabbits. Another group of sauces include those from plant sources. A third group [is] made with different fish. Meat sauces are the most ancient.
>
> As early as during the Zhou dynasty (1045–256 BCE), there is a record of an old meat sauce recipe. It appears in the *Li Ji*, a classical Chinese book compiled during the time of the Western Han dynasty (206–25 BCE). It tells about earlier times when it was used. In the *Li Ji* there are two kinds of meat sauces. One is made without bones and called *hai*. The other is made with bones and called *ni*.[15]

The difference between those last meat sauces curiously mirrors our distinction between stock (made from bones) and broth (made from meat).

The sauce cookery of other Asian cultures—much of which has developed from contact with Chinese techniques—is heavily dependent on preserved ingredients. Dried, salted, and fermented foods practically define these cuisines.

In ancient China, most people were poor and had a hard life. They cherished and treasured food, and they learned how to preserve it. Their efforts led to advanced preservation techniques, and in the process, they learned to make many fermented sauces using different materials.

The sauce made from soybeans—namely, soy sauce—is not as old as meat sauces, but today it is the king of all fermented seasonings. Many sauces change the flavor and appearance of foods, as do soy sauces. Different ones make for a large variety of different food tastes including all sauces from soybeans.

Fish sauces also played and still play important roles in people's lives in China. This is especially true for those who lived in the Yangzi and Yellow River regions. While Chinese fish sauces are also ancient, they are newer than meat sauces, and they have their own unique features. They are generally referred to as *yu hai*. Some fish sauces are recorded in the *Zhou Li*, but these were not as popular.[16]

Asian fish sauces are similar to, but not exactly the same as, Roman *liquamen*—but, like soy sauce, they serve the same culinary functions: providing salt and umami.

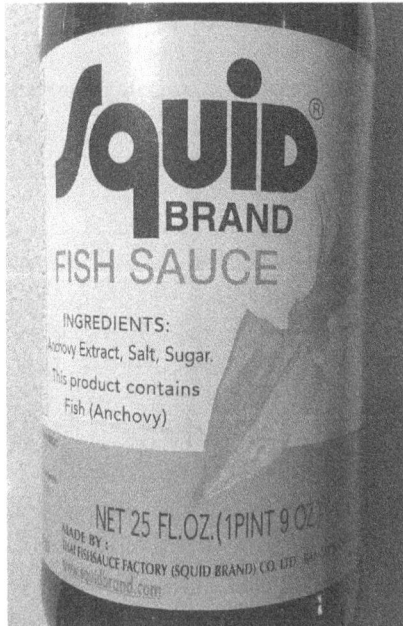

A popular brand of fish sauce—which is not, as one might reasonably expect, made from squid. *Source:* Gary Allen

2

OLD WINE IN NEW BOTTLES

Before the 1960s—when Julia Child's TV show introduced many Americans to *real* French food—many people thought that French food was anything covered with too much sauce. This is ironic, since Americans slathered sauces on most of their meals—meals that they believed to be red-blooded American, through and through. They never imagined that ketchup, mustard, gravy, barbecue sauce, A.1., salad dressing, Tabasco, mayonnaise, and Worcestershire sauce had anything in common with fussy, overdressed French cuisine.

What so many didn't realize was that French culinary traditions governed a great many of our eating habits. The structure of our meals, the organization of restaurant kitchens and their staffs, and even our most ordinary dishes (often accompanied by flour-thickened gravies) have all been influenced by

Nineteenth-century ad for Worcestershire sauce. *Source:* Public domain our French forebears. If we are to understand our use of, and relation to, the world's vast pantry of sauces, we really need to begin in France.

There is a popular notion that French cuisine did not begin to flower until Catherine de Medici brought the cooking of the Italian Renaissance with her in 1533. This fallacy becomes apparent if we glance at *Le viandier de Taillevent*. This fourteenth-century cookbook—like the one attributed to Apicius—is associated with someone who may, or may not, have been involved in its production. For this book, Guillaume Tirel (aka Taillevent), like Apicius, largely collected preexisting recipes. Unlike Apicius (who had been dead for centuries before his book was assembled), Tirel may have added later parts to a book that first appeared a decade or so before he was born. Plagiarism was not considered a fault back then (and copyright had yet to be invented); it was actually prized as a measure of an author's erudition.

Many of Tirel's sauces were based on the drippings, juices, and liquids in which the main ingredients cooked. The technique used was much like that of the sauces from ancient Mesopotamia. Tirel contributed a degree of refinement to the evolution of sauces. While his sauces were still thickened with bits of stale bread (or eggs or puréed vegetables), forcing the liquid and lumps through a drum-shaped, muslin-lined strainer (a *tamis*) yielded a smoother, more luxurious sauce than was previously possible.

No attempt was made to impose logical order on the collection of recipes, other than grouping them in the cookbook—as in Apicius—by usage or by variations of seasoning employed. The only category for sauces that appears in Tirel's table of contents is a group of six unboiled sauces. One, for cameline sauce, was thickened with bread and had the typical spice-heavy flavors of the Middle Ages. It incorporated cinnamon, cloves, ginger, grains of paradise, mace, and long pepper, brightened with a bit of vinegar. He added a second version perfumed with garlic. Here are a couple more examples of Tirel's sauces (note that the first one uses nuts as a thickener, in Arabic/medieval fashion, but both are—in more modern fashion—strained free of any lumpiness).

Historic Recipe: 85. Yellow Sauce

A Yellow Sauce for cold fish fried in oil without flour. Grind almonds, steep in wine (mostly) and verjuice, sieve, and boil. Grind ginger, cloves, grains of paradise and a bit of saffron, and steep in your broth. Boil well with some sugar. It should be very thick.[1]

Historic Recipe: 218. Must Sauce

Take some grapes from the bunch, peel them in a pan, and boil them on the fire for half a quarter of an hour. Add just a bit of red wine if you do not have enough grapes. Let them cool, and strain through cheesecloth.

For four platters, take two ounces of cinnamon, two ounces of sugar and a half ounce of ginger, and strain everything except the sugar through cheesecloth. If you do not have grapes, use mulberries.[2]

Despite the work of chefs like Tirel, the French did not immediately adopt the notion of haute cuisine seen, for example, in the works of Bartolomeo Scappi. Montaigne even ridiculed what he saw as the absurd hyperbole of an Italian chef in describing his cuisine: "He expounded to me a distinction in appetites: that which exists before eating, that after the second and third courses; how sometimes simply to gratify it, sometimes to arouse and stimulate it; the care of his sauces, first in general, and the going into particulars as to the qualities of the ingredients and their effect."[3] He then made certain his contempt for such nonsense was clear: "And all this inflated with rich and magnificent words and even such as are used in discoursing about government of an empire."[4] French cuisine might have been on its way to becoming *haute*, but it was not yet ready to be accorded the status of art, nor was it a subject worthy of study. It certainly did not yet deserve the kind of detailed discourse in which even casual eaters engage today. Montaigne would be rolling in his grave—with laughter—to learn that volumes, such as the one you are reading, even exist, let alone that it is just one of thousands of similar books.

Tirel's cookbook may have been the first French volume of "gourmet" cookery, but it was not the first food book written in France. That honor goes to Anthimus's *De observatione ciborum* (On the observance of foods). Anthimus was a fifth-century Byzantine, stationed for a time as an ambassador in Gaul, where he wrote the book. It was not really a cookbook so much as a guide to healthy eating, one that drew heavily on humoral notions of medicine.

The humors were four bodily fluids (and their corresponding temperaments)—black bile, yellow bile, phlegm, and blood—and the balance between them controlled one's health, according to the writings of Hippocrates. Various foodstuffs were prescribed to restore humoral equilibrium, but sugar was thought to be in perfect balance, which might explain its presence in so many recipes of the day. Humoral medicine (and related diets) dominated until, during the Renaissance, Galen's writings replaced it.

Anthimus frequently mentioned sauces, but usually only to add ingredients to unspecified sauces (of which, presumably, his readers were already aware). Like many popular modern cookbooks, his focused on health—at least as it was understood at the time. Also, like writers of many of today's diet-based cookbooks, he was fond of listing all the foods one must never eat. The puritanical killjoy approach to gastronomy is hardly new.

Historical Recipe: Lentils

Lentils are good when washed and carefully boiled in fresh water. Make sure that the first lot of water is poured away, and a second lot of hot water added as required, but not too much, and then boil the lentils slowly on the hearth. When they are cooked, add for flavour a little vinegar, together with the addition of that spice which is called Syrian sumach. Sprinkle a spoonful of this spice over the lentils while they are still on the fire, and stir in well. Take the lentils off the fire and serve. You can add a good spoonful of oil from unripe olives to the second water while the lentils are still cooking, as well as one or two spoonfuls of coriander including the roots—not ground but whole—and a pinch of salt for seasoning.[5]

The offer of possible variations, giving the cook a chance to express his or her tastes, has a modern flavor. Distinctly less modern was Anthimus's opinion about cheesy sauces: "Whoever eats baked or boiled cheese has no need of another poison, because after the oil has been separated pure stones are produced; nor should it be boiled, because it becomes salty when the oil is lost. To prove this, boil some cheese, take it from the fire, put it away to cool, and it grows stonelike or salty. Similarly, what benefit can cheese confer when ingested after being baked, except to produce pure stones?"[6]

Also in keeping with tradition, his book makes clear that Roman approaches to food were still in effect after the fall of the empire—including the use of spices, which continued well into the medieval period.

At roughly the same time as Tirel's book (1324), a collection of Catalonian recipes was published, anonymously, as *The Book of Sent Soví*. The little book contained seventy-two recipes, at least a dozen of which are for sauces (the number is approximate, because some other recipes, such as gelatin and various purées, might have served as sauces but are not so described). *Sent Soví*'s take on cameline sauce is more detailed than many medieval recipes—though the recipes are clearly not written in a form modern cook might recognize.

Historic Recipe: Salsa Camillina

If you want to make camel sauce, make almond milk out of unpeeled almonds with a good chicken broth. After that, mince the chicken livers and blend them with the milk. Set it to boil, and put in sugar and pomegranate wine or red vinegar or verjuice—however, always be sure that it is red verjuice—and cinnamon as the largest portion, and ginger and other good spices and pepper, and the same with cloves, grains of paradise, nutmeg, two types of pepper, and white sugar. Let it boil a lot, and, when it is well cooked, flavor it with salt, spices, and verjuice and sweetening. And, if you want, you can put in a couple of roasted or boiled chickens or capons, which you should leave a while with the almond milk. And put in a lot of the roasted chicken's grease.[7]

This is a typically complex medieval recipe, combining sweet and savory, with lots of costly spices—plus a few forms of sugar, which was imported and treated as a spice. The anonymous author, like Anthimus, made many of his recipes adaptable for health reasons (though the medieval idea of which foodstuffs were beneficial to one's health differs somewhat from ours). This recipe shares some of the characteristics of our pestos or *chimichurris*:

Historic Recipe: Salsa Verd

If you want to make green sauce, take parsley leaves, and wash the tender parts, and dry them in the sun, or without sun. Grind them well with cinnamon and ginger, and cloves, pepper and toasted hazelnuts. Put in a good measure of each ingredient and taste it, and if you see one thing is more evident than another, balance it to be equal. [A]nd one can put in bread, toasted and soaked in vinegar. Put in honey or sugar for a delicate or sick person.[8]

Tirel's *Le viandier of Taillevent* was so successful that it was soon flattered by imitation, not least by *The Forme of Cury*. That compendium of medieval dishes was assembled in the last decade of the fourteenth century, allegedly by the kitchen staff of Richard II. Its take on cameline sauce is typi-cal of the recipes purloined from Tirel.

Historic Recipe: Sawse Camelyne

Take Raysouns of Coraunce. & kyrnels of notys. & crustes of brede & pow-dour of gyngur clowes flour of canel. bray it wel togyder and do it yerto. salt it, temper it up with vynegur. and serue it forth.[9]

Translated for modern cooks, it reads something like this:

Take raisins of Corinth [what we call dried currants], shelled nutmeats, bread crusts, and powdered ginger, cloves, and cinnamon. Pound them together well, adjust seasoning with salt, brighten with vinegar, and serve it forth.

An equally confusing recipe is this one for a roast goose (with rough translation to follow):

Historic Recipe: Sawse Madame

Take sawge. persel. ysope. and saueray. quinces. and peeres, garlek and Grapes. and fylle the gees flerwith. and sowe the hole flat no grece come out. and roost hem wel. and kepe the grece flat fallith flerof. take galytyne and grece and do in a possynet, whan the gees buth rosted ynowh; take an smyte hem on pecys. and flat tat is withinne and do it in a possynet and put flerinne wyne if it be to thyk. do flerto powdour of galyngale. powdour douce and salt and boyle the sawse and dresse fle Gees in disshes and lay fle sowe onoward.[10]

Not too easy to read, is it? Perhaps this is simpler:

Take sage, parsley, hyssop, summer savory, quinces, and pears, garlic and grapes. Fill the geese therewith and sew the hole shut so to avoid losing too much fat. Roast them well and reserve any fat that accumulates. Take galytyne [sauce made with meat juices, thickened with bread] and grease and place in a small pot, when the geese have roasted enough; chop them into pieces. Add wine to the small pot if the sauce is too thick. Add powdered galangal, sweet powder [a variable mixed spice usually containing ginger, cinnamon, clove, and nutmeg—similar to our pumpkin pie spice], and salt. Boil the sauce and place the geese in serving dishes, pouring the sauce over them.

In 1508, Wynkyn de Worde published *The Boke of Keruynge* (The book of carving), a collection of instructions for the tableside carving of meats. This duty was one of the privileges of men of nobility—and nobility was one of the rewards of being a successful warrior. While noblemen were expected to master the courtly art of carving, sauce making would have been beneath them. Nonetheless, *The Boke of Keruynge* is careful to point out the proper sauces that should accompany its bewildering menagerie of roasted beasts.

> Mustard is good with brawn, chine of beef, bacon and mutton. Verjuice is good with boiled chickens and capon; swan with chawdrons; ribs of beef with garlic, mustard, pepper, verjuice; ginger sauce with lamb, pig and fawn; mustard and sugar with pheasant, partridge and coney; sauce gameline with herons, egret, plover and crane. With whimbrel and curlew: salt, sugar and water of tame; with bustard, shoveller and bittern: sauce gameline. Woodcock, lapwing, lark, quail, martin, venison and snipe with white salt. Sparrows and thrushes with salt and cinnamon. Thus each meat has its appropriate sauce.[11]

Chawdron is a sauce of swan stock and wine flavored with spices (cloves, ginger, and pepper) and salt and thickened with swan's blood and bread. Gameline is a variant spelling of cameline. A whimbrel is a curlew-like shorebird, and coney is just another word for rabbit.

Lords and ladies of the sixteenth century did not limit their protein consumption to beasts of the land and air. Waters, both salt and fresh, teemed with creatures, large and small, each of which called for its particular sauce.

> Mustard is good with salt herring, salt fish, salt conger, salmon, sparling, salt eel and ling. Vinegar is good with salt porpoise, salt tuna, salt sturgeon, thorpole and salt whale; galantine with lamprey; verjuice with roach, dace, bream, mullet, bass, flounders, sole, crab; powdered cinnamon with chub. With thornback, herring, houndfish, haddock, whiting and cod: vinegar, powdered cinnamon and ginger. Green sauce is good with green fish, halibut, cuttlefish and fresh turbot. Do not put your green sauce away, it is good with mustard.[12]

Galantine, in the Middle Ages, did not refer to the showpiece of today's *garde manger*. It was a sauce made from the spiced jelly released when cooking eels or lampreys, thickened with breadcrumbs or other bread-thickened sauces, and flavored with galingale (galangal, *Cyperus longus*).

The desire for systematic thought and the imposition of logical structure on the world really took off with the Enlightenment. Following the *Novum organum* of Francis Bacon (1561–1626), the encyclopedists, under Denis Diderot (1713–1784), assembled the massive *Encyclopédie, ou dictionnaire raisonné des sciences, des arts et des métiers*, and Linnaeus (1707–1778) invented biological taxonomy. The desire for order—and to understand the underlying principles that reveal connections between everything we experience or help us to distinguish between similar things—was clearly in the air during the so-called long eighteenth century.

This led to the evolution of the natural philosophy of the ancients into something like what we call science. Alchemy, for example, matured into chemistry. Whereas the alchemists wanted to extract the essence of things—essentially to discard the gross corporeal substance in favor of its rarified spirit (the retort, used for distilling, is practically a symbol for the alchemist's art)—cooks of the sixteenth century began to see things differently: "The French reined in alchemy to serve the sensual table, literally debasing the spiritual essences. Similarly, the new science reined in and co-opted alchemy by taking over its technological base while jettisoning its cosmological assumptions. Cookery forced Paracelsian ideas into sensual submission, much as science checked them by cutting the occult web of influences."[13]

In cooking, recipes had been collected for more than a millennium with little thought about how they related to one another. The minds of the Enlightenment must have seen that as a fundamental weakness. Consider Diderot's entry on sauce:

> Liquid composition in which cooks cook various types of dishes, or which they make separately to eat with meat when they are cooked. Our modern sauces are rather known, but perhaps it will be helpful to find here some of the cooking sauces of our ancestors that Monsieur Sauval has described in his antiquities of Paris. These sauces are yellow sauce, hot sauce, compote sauce, mustard sauce or galantine, sauce rapée, green sauce, and finally camelaine.
>
> Yellow sauce was made with white pepper, which our forefathers named jaunet. It was part of a number of hot sauces. In compote sauce, black pepper is used.
>
> Mustard sauce or galantine was made with the root of this plant, which our botanists no longer know. It was perhaps nothing other than the horse-

radish we presently put into our sauces, which is neither less hot nor less spicy than galantine.

Sauce rapée was made with verjuice of grapes or green currants.

Green sauce (which we still know) had among other ingredients ginger and verjuice, and was made green with parsley juice or green wheat. Next white bread crumbs were added.

Regarding camelaine, which took its name from a medicinal plant we no longer know, it was made with cinnamon, ginger, cloves, mustard seed, wine, verjuice, bread, and vinegar. As such it was the most complex of all the sauces of that time.

The right to make and sell sauces once belonged to merchant-spicers, who consequently took the name spicers-apothecaries-saucers. But since then, the name and the product have passed to master-vinegarists, who still at present count among their qualities that of master-saucer.

Sauce Robert, as a cook's term, is onions seasoned with mustard and cooked in the fat of a pork loin or other cut which has been mixed with the sauce dabbed on it.

Cooks also call green sauce a sauce made with green wheat, toast, pepper, and salt, all ground together and passed through a cloth.[14]

Sauce Robert is the only sauce that is even recognizable to us today. According to legend, it was invented in the early seventeenth century and gets its name from saucier Robert Vinot. It is significant for its incorporation of butter, which was to become an iconic ingredient in French sauce cookery. "Butter is not found in recipes for sauces in the fourteenth- and fifteenth-century cookery works from England, France, or Italy, but it does begin to appear there in the first half of the sixteenth century. Eight percent of the recipes for sauces in *Le Livre fort excellent* contain butter. It appears in 39 percent of La Varenne's sauce recipes and climbs to 55 percent of Menon's in *La Cuisière bourgoise*."[15]

François Pierre La Varenne, in *Le cuisinier françois* (1651), began to formulate a system of sauces that broke with heavily spiced medieval traditions. Roux, made with flour and lard, was his preferred thickener. He never achieved anything like the taxonomy we'd prefer, but his book was, after all, a cookbook—an Enlightenment-era cookbook, but a cookbook nonetheless.

As a first attempt to grapple with the complexities of sauce taxonomy, Diderot's entry is barely acceptable for our use. Not only are most of the sauces mentioned unfamiliar to us, but the entry itself also lacks the kind of intellectual rigor we would expect from, say, Linnaeus.

We must look elsewhere for a comprehensive approach to the classification of sauces.

3

NINETEENTH CENTURY

Fortunately, others have attempted to improve (or systematize) cooking, each time making small gains.

CARÊME

Antoine Carême (1784–1833), a giant in the history of French cooking, rose to prominence at a time when postrevolutionary France was literally building itself anew. It's no accident that he was famous for the architectural splendor of his creations or that he wanted to build a culinary system that reflected a modern taste for order and reason. France's political revolution and Carême's culinary revolution are both descended from the ideals of the Enlightenment.

In his 1854 book *L'art de la cuisine française au dix-neuvième siecle* (The art of French cooking in the nineteenth century), he attempted to impose order on the chaos of French sauces. With characteristic smugness, he asserted that French sauces were superior to those of any other nation. He listed dozens of them (some derived—and improved through "Frenchification"—from non-Gallic sources: "sauce italienne, sauce vénitienne, sauce hollandaise, sauce russe, sauce polonaise, sauce portugaise, sauce milanaise," and on and on) but wanted to do more than compile a Diderot-like catalog. He was the first to understand that there might be a way to do more than assemble a listing of the endless variety of sauces. He wanted to understand the unifying structure behind all that complexity.

He proposed four *grandes sauces*, from which, he asserted, all the others could be derived. *Sauce velouté* is made today from reduced veal or chicken stock, using raw bones, thickened with white roux of flour and butter. Carême's version:

Ingredients

1 oz.	butter
1 oz.	flour
3 glassfuls	stock—preferably veal
to taste	salt and pepper
pinch	nutmeg
pinch	ground ginger

Method

1. Melt the butter and stir in the flour.
2. Add gradually the stock, ginger, nutmeg, and seasoning.
3. Bring to a boil and simmer, skimming occasionally, until reduced by half.
4. The sauce should now be thick but light and creamy. Add cream to turn this into the white glaze for chicken *à l'ivoire*.[1]

Sauce béchamel was once made by adding heavy cream to velouté but is prepared today from scalded milk, thickened with a pale roux of flour and butter. Carême's version:

Ingredients

½ oz.	butter
2 Tbsp.	flour
½ pint	milk
to taste	salt and pepper
to taste	grated nutmeg
1	shallot, stuck with a clove
bouquet garnie	

Method

1. Heat the butter and stir in the flour and add, gradually, the milk, shallot, nutmeg, and bouquet garnie.

2. Simmer very slowly for 20 minutes, remove bouquet garnie and shallot before serving.[2]

Sauce espagnole is made from reduced veal stock, using roasted bones, thickened with slightly browned roux of flour and butter. Carême's version:

Ingredients

2 oz.	butter
1 oz.	flour
1 pint	dark meat stock
bouquet garnie	
1 oz.	tomato purée

Method

1. Melt the butter, stir in the flour and cook gently on a low heat until well browned.
2. Add the stock and stir until it thickens.
3. Add the bouquet garnie and simmer half an hour. By this time the sauce will have reduced.
4. Remove the bouquet garnie, add the tomato purée and simmer another five minutes.[3]

Sauce allemande is essentially an enriched velouté, substituting egg yolks and heavy cream for the pale roux of béchamel. Its richness is brightened today with a few drops of lemon juice. Carême's version:

Ingredients

1 oz.	butter
1 oz.	flour
½ pint	boiling water
to taste	salt and pepper
1	egg
3 drops	wine vinegar

Method

1. Melt the butter, add the flour and then the boiling water and seasoning.
2. Off the heat, whisk well the egg and vinegar and add gradually to the sauce whilst whisking. Do not reboil.[4]

Obviously these sauces are but slight variations on velouté, basically exchanging the base liquid and varying the degree to which the roux is cooked before being added. The technique is essentially the same: they're starch-thickened sauces, as ancient and firmly rooted in tradition as anything from Mesopotamia.

Unlike the celebrity chefs who would follow him, Carême did not cook in restaurants. He often worked for royalty, in immense kitchens, and some of his prestige was a consequence of his close association with the high and mighty.[5] His culinary fame marks a transition from the great private chefs of the distant past (like Guillaume Tirel) and more modern examples (like Auguste Escoffier). Today's celebrity chefs generally come from the restaurant industry.

While Carême's organization might make practical sense in a professional kitchen's procedures, it feels arbitrary and incomplete. One need only consider *sauce mayonnaise* (which Carême wrote about at length elsewhere but failed to include among his *grandes sauces*) to see the limitations of his system. Raymond Sokolov writes in *The Saucier's Apprentice*, "Some people. . . say mayonnaise, others mahonnaise, still others bayonnaise. . . . Carême was convinced that his etymology made the most sense: [his preferred] magnonaise came from the verb 'manier,' to handle or work, which he argued, was exactly what one did to produce a good mayonnaise."[6] The fact that he recognized mayonnaise's distinguishing attribute to be its *process* rather than its ingredients (not to mention an entirely different method of thickening) should have led him to rethink his sauce taxonomy. But he didn't. It was a valiant attempt but hardly the best solution to the problem he set for himself.

BRILLAT-SAVARIN

Jean Antheleme Brillat-Savarin (1755–1826), whose name is practically synonymous with gastronomy—fine dining and especially *thinking* about fine dining—completed *The Physiology of Taste: Or, Transcendental Gastronomy* only months before his death. Had he not written it, he would barely be remembered today. The book mentions sauce just three times, twice merely in passing. However, Book 6, "On Food in General," discusses two ancient Roman sauces: *muria* and *garum*.

> The first was nothing but the brine of the tunny, or rather the juice which flowed from it when it was salted. *Garum*, which was more costly, is much less well known to us. It is believed that it was made by pressing the seasoned entrails of the scomber or mackerel, but if that were so its high price would not be justified. There is reason to believe that it was an imported sauce, perhaps that soy which comes to us from India and which is known to be the result of letting certain fishes ferment with mushrooms.[7]

Brillat-Savarin was certainly mistaken about *garum* being imported (the Romans had *garum* "factories" all around the Mediterranean) and about it being soy sauce. Neither came from India, nor was *garum* made from fish and mushrooms. He was closer to the mark when thinking about what these sauces had in common.

One of Brillat-Savarin's most brilliant "discoveries" was of something that doesn't exist, despite his conviction that it did. His "osmazome" was to gastronomy what "phlogiston" was to early physical science: an invented term for something unobservable in order to explicate the inexplicable.

> Osmazome is that preeminently sapid part of meat which is soluble in cold water, and which differs completely from the extractive part of the meat, which is soluble only in water that is boiling.
>
> It is osmazome which gives all their value to good soups; it is osmazome which, as it browns, makes the savory reddish tinge in sauces and the crisp coating on roasted meat, finally it's from the osmazome that comes the special tangy juices of venison and game.[8]

A lot of Brillat-Savarin's "science" was little more than wishful thinking, but it foreshadowed two actual scientific discoveries: the Maillard reaction (discovered in 1910 by Louis Camille Maillard), which provides the tasty browning on roasted meats and other foods, and umami (discovered in 1908 by Kikunae Ikeda), the savory taste that was only proven to be the fifth basic taste in 2001. As we shall see, the qualities that he assigned to "osmazome" are essential to many of the sauces we'll be discussing here.

SOYER AND BOTTLED SAUCES

The nineteenth century was a great time for inventors, and Alexis Benoist Soyer (1810–1858) was a prime example. Soyer, another early celebrity chef, is best remembered as a kitchen innovator. His kitchens featured gas stoves and ovens, the temperatures of which could be set, and a precursor of the modern refrigerator (it was not an ice box but cooled its contents through the evaporation of water).

Soyer was one of the first chefs to confront the problem of feeding large numbers of people in inconvenient circumstances. In 1847, he developed portable stoves that could be set up in impromptu soup kitchens to help

An engraving of Soyer by Henry Bryan Hall, 1858. *Source:* Public domain

feed the victims of Ireland's potato famine. He improved on the Soyer Stove for use in the Crimean War (1853–1856), refining the one he had created to deal with the Great Irish Famine in order to feed troops in the field. His traveling kitchen included an ironclad horse-drawn cart with stove and a hundred-gallon-capacity steam digester—a forerunner of today's pressure cookers. It weighed a ton but was vastly more efficient than any other field kitchen used by armies of the day.

He wrote a number of cookbooks, mostly meant to modernize cooks' methods. One book, *The Gastronomic Regenerator* (1846), sorts sauces into large and small sauces, a system that was roughly equivalent to mother and daughter sauces. He numbered all his recipes so that a cook could easily construct a given "small sauce" from one or more of his other recipes. He provided some basic rules for sauce makers:

> All kinds of fish sauce should be thicker for boiled fish than for broiled or fried.
>   Brown sauce should be a little thinnish and the colour of a horse-chesnut [*sic*].
>   White sauce should be of the colour of ivory, and thicker than brown sauce.
>   Cream, or Dutch sauce, must be rather thick, and cannot be too white.
>   Demi-glace requires to be rather thin, but yet sufficiently reduced to envelope any pieces of meat, game, poultry, &c., with which it is served.[9]

Today we tend to think of Italian sauces as "red," being based on tomatoes. The very first Italian tomato sauce appeared in Antonio Latini's *Lo scalco alla moderna* (The modern steward) in 1692. It was based on a tomato sauce from Spain.

Historic Recipe: Salsa di Pomodoro alla Spagnola

Take half a dozen ripe tomatoes and roast them in embers, and when they are charred, carefully remove the skin, and mince them finely with a knife. Add as many onions, finely minced, as desired; chiles, also finely minced; and a small amount of thyme. After mixing everything together, add a little salt, oil, and vinegar as needed. It is a very tasty sauce, for boiled dishes or anything else.[10]

By the nineteenth century Soyer was listing two versions of *sauce à l'italienne*, neither of which were red or looked like anything you might find on spaghetti or pizza. The modular nature of his recipes is quite apparent.

Historic Recipe: No. 30. Sauce à l'Italienne

Put two tablespoonfuls of chopped onions and one of chopped eschalots in a stewpan with three tablespoonfuls of salad oil, stir them ten minutes over a sharp fire; then add a wine-glassful of sherry, a pint of brown sauce (No. 1), and half a pint of consommé (No. 134), set it over a sharp fire until it boils, then place it at the corner, let it simmer ten minutes, skim off all the oil which it will throw up, then place it over the fire, stir with a spoon, reducing it until it adheres to the back of it, then add a teaspoonful of chopped parsley, a tablespoonful of chopped mushrooms, a little sugar, salt if required, and finish with the juice of half a lemon.[11]

Historic Recipe: No. 31. Sauce à l'Italienne (white)

Italian sauce for any description of fish, white meat, or poultry, must be made white, which is done by following the directions of the preceding receipts, only substituting white sauce (No. 7) for the brown, and finishing with three spoonfuls of cream.[12]

He does, however, follow with a red sauce—but it is decidedly French in character and preparation, and it would never be confused with spaghetti sauce.

Historic Recipe: No. 37. Sauce aux Tomates

Procure two dozen ripe tomatoes, take out the stalk, squeeze out the juice and the seeds, then put them into a stewpan with a little salt, stew until tender, and drain them upon a sieve; then, in another stewpan, put two onions, part of a carrot, and a turnip, all cut in very thin slices, with a bunch of parsley, two sprigs of thyme, two bay-leaves, two cloves, a blade of mace, a clove of garlic, two ounces of lean uncooked ham, and a quarter of a pound of butter; place the stewpan over a moderate fire, stir the mirepoix round occasionally, until the vegetables are tender, then add the tomatoes, stir them over the fire another minute, then stir in six ounces of flour, and add two quarts of consommé (No. 134); boil altogether twenty-five minutes, keeping it stirred, season it with a little salt, sugar, and cayenne pepper, then rub it through a tammie; put it into another stewpan, set it over the fire, when boiling place it at the corner, let simmer ten minutes, skim well, then pour it in a basin, and use where directed. If no tomatoes, use two bottles of preserved tomatoes. If too thick, dilute it with a little more consommé.[13]

Through his travels, Soyer learned a lot about the food of the eastern Mediterranean. He adapted some of the dishes he encountered there—in the way the French typically adapt foreign recipes, with results that barely resemble their inspiration (though, in this case, Soyer incorporates several British prepared sauces as well). For example:

Historic Recipe: No. 64. Sauce à la Beyrout

Put a tablespoonful of chopped onions into a stewpan with one of Chili vinegar and one of common vinegar, eighteen spoonfuls of melted butter, four of brown gravy, two of mushroom catsup, and two of Harvey sauce; then place it over the fire, keep stirring until boiling, then place it at the corner of the stove, let it simmer five minutes, skim it well, then place it again over the fire and stir until it adheres to the back of the spoon, then add two tablespoonfuls of essence of anchovies, and half a teaspoonful of sugar; it is then ready to serve. The above is a fish sauce, but may be used for meat or poultry by substituting white sauce (No. 7) for melted butter (No. 71).[14]

Soyer was very interested in sauces that boosted levels of umami—or, as Brillat-Savarin would have said, "osmazome." Interestingly enough, both looked to the sauces of the ancient Romans for guidance. According to Soyer, "In all ages and countries. . . sauces of various kinds have been an accompaniment. With the Romans, in the time of Lucullus, great care was observed in their preparation; amongst others which they used, and the most celebrated, was the Garum and the Muria. The Garum was the sauce the most esteemed and the most expensive, its composition is unknown. This is a subject well worth the attention of the epicures of the present day."[15] Like Brillat-Savarin, Soyer made some guesses about these sauces' ingredients. He suspected mushrooms and mackerel but was vague about their species. He was certainly right about mushrooms and salted fish being sources of "osmazome," even if mushrooms weren't needed to provide it in *garum* and *muria*. In 1853, he even patented something called "Soyer's Osmazome Food," which was never actually marketed. Soyer's patent application includes instructions for making what appears to have been concentrated beef stock: "Separate the fibrous part from the gravy, which is reduced by boiling, and afterwards deposited in bottles, or other receptacles, which are subjected to heat, and sealed, and in which it will keep till required."[16] He was, unfortunately, somewhat ahead of his time (John Lawson Johnston created Bovril in the 1870s).

What is demi-glace, ultimately, but a form of concentrated beef stock? Here's Soyer's recipe for that unctuous substance, the foundation of so many sauces—or, as he put it, "This sauce is the real key to cooking a good and ceremonious dinner":

Historic Recipe: Demi-Glaze

Put a pint of brown sauce in a middle-sized stewpan, add to it half a pint of broth or consommé, put it on the stove, stir with wooden spoon, let it boil as fast as possible, take the scum off which will rise to the surface, reduce it until it adheres lightly to the spoon, pass it through a sieve or tammy into a basin, stir now and then until cold, to prevent a skin forming on the top, put it by until wanted for use. It will keep for a week in winter, by adding half a gill of white broth every other day, and giving it a boil; the addition of a tablespoonful of tomatos [*sic*], gives it a beautiful color.[17]

Nicolas-François Appert had invented canning in corked glass bottles only in 1811, and Soyer began selling bottles of three of his prepared condiments (Soyer's Diamond Sauce, Kalos Geusis, and Versailles Sauce) in the mid-1840s through a company called William Clayton & Company. Apparently the Clayton firm had poor marketing skills; nothing came of the ventures. Then, in 1848, he connected with a couple of young men, Edmund Crosse and Thomas Blackwell, who had just purchased a company that had previously, as West & Wyatt, produced jams, jellies, and preserves. They opened a shop on the southwest corner of Soho Square and bottled their line of products at the nearby former West & Wyatt factory.

Their first collaborations were Soyer's Sauce, offered in two flavors—mild for the ladies and hot for the gentlemen. Crosse & Blackwell had bought the licenses to all the Clayton sauces, and it's possible that these two new sauces were reworkings of the recipe for Soyer's Diamond Sauce, which had been advertised as a perfect condiment for "cold or hot meat, poultry, game, etc."[18] Like many modern bottled sauces, Soyer's sauce for gentlemen came with "recipes" on the label—the chef's own recommendations:

For any kind of cold meat, game, and poultry, use it in moderation as it is. For mutton, lamb, pork, and steaks, when properly boiled and seasoned, pour one tablespoon or more, according to the quantity of meat, which you turn over in the dish with a fork several times, than you will have a most excellent gravy. In any sort of hash it is a very great improvement. For made dishes or *entreés* put four tablespoonfuls of brown sauce to six of broth, and when quite hot add two tablespoonfuls of Soyer's Sauce; just boil it, and pour over your *entreés*.

For general purposes put eight tablespoonfuls of water into a stewpan; when boiling, add four ditto of the sauce, half an ounce of fresh butter mixed with a quarter of an ounce of flour, stir quickly on the fire, add if required a little salt, boil one minute, and pour over your dish of meat, game, or poultry.[19]

A year later, Crosse & Blackwell released Soyer's Relish, "an entirely new and economical condiment, adapted for all kinds of viands, which, by those who have tasted, has been pronounced *perfect.*"[20] It was extremely success-ful, despite having a distinct—and distinctly un-Victorian—garlicky char-acter. A review in *The Observer* raved, "At present we do not know of any person who administers more assiduously and effectively to our corporeal wants—at any rate, to our most craving of them—than the renowned Soyer. ... [W]e see him now compounding a sauce, which undoubtedly will prove a 'relish' to the most used-up of palates."[21]

In 1853, Crosse & Blackwell debuted Soyer's Aromatic Mustard, "a most exquisite combination of the genuine Mustard seed with various aro-matic substances: infinitely superior to all preparations of Mustard."[22]

By way of maintaining his character for novelty of invention in the gastro-nomic art, M. Soyer has recently added another relish to his already numerous dainties, with which to tickle the palates of his numerous patrons. This is a condiment in the shape of aromatic mustard, which is decidedly an improve-ment to the dinner table, and imparts an excellent flavour to meat and poultry, whether hot or cold. It is not for the uninitiated to seek to dive into the secrets of M. Soyer's inventions; suffice it to say, that they ought to be satisfied with tasting the aromatic mustard, and approving of so delicate and relishing an addition to their "dainty dishes." Doubtless it will go the round of the festive board, and ensure for itself the appropriate motto of "cut and come again."[23]

It's probably only a coincidence that Soyer was born in Meauxen-Brie, a re-gion so famous for its mustard that Brillat-Savarin is said to have exclaimed, "If it isn't Meaux, it isn't mustard!"[24]

Soyer combined his eastern experiences with his obvious penchant for technological tinkering to create a vaguely more authentic condiment. Crosse & Blackwell marketed his Soyer's Sultana Sauce, the first bottled brown sauce and the ancestor of countless others, such as American A.1. and Jamaican Pickapeppa. It appeared in 1857, and its advertisement boasted that it was "a most refreshing and pleasing stimulant to the appetite, composed principally of Turkish condiments combined with various culinary productions of the East. It is an exquisite relish with Fish, Meat, Poultry, and Game, and forms a valuable addition to Soups, Minces, Hashes, Stews, Meat Pies and Puddings, as well as to Salads of every description. To Steaks and Chops it imparts a highly delicious and aromatic flavour."[25] Victorian marketing might sound like the spiel of a snake-oil barker, but when combined with his celebrity status—which he worked very hard to promote—it was effective. While not the first of his commercially produced bottled sauces, it was certainly the best received.

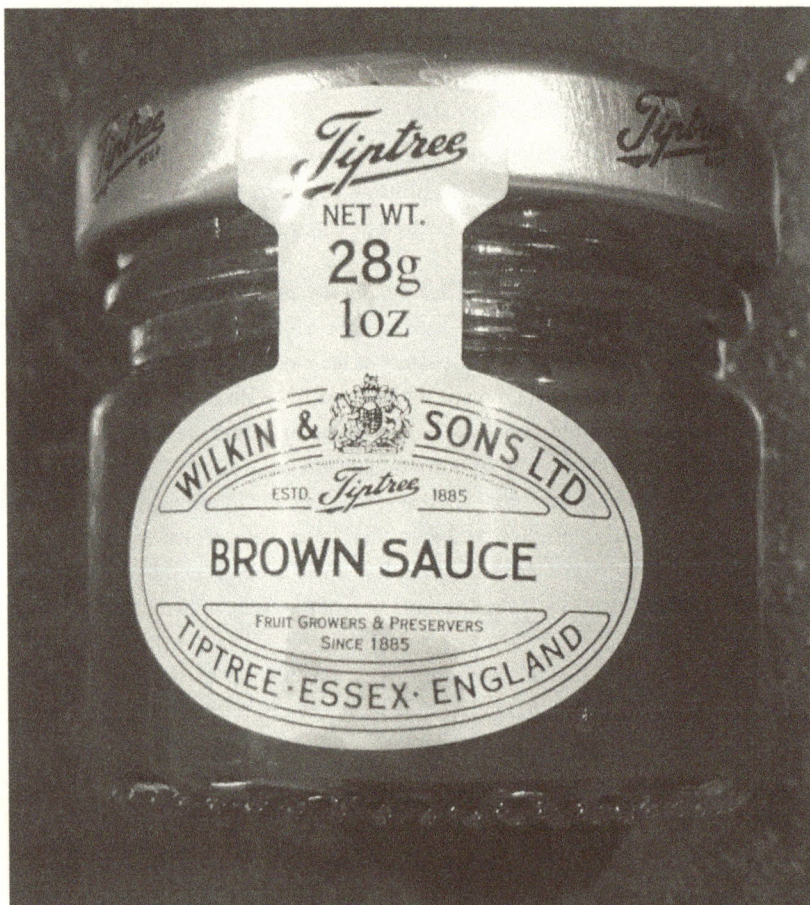

Brown sauce. *Source:* Gary Allen

Soyer's mass-market approach to the licensing, production, and distribution of bottled sauces predates the efforts of American entrepreneur Henry John Heinz by more than a decade. Like Heinz's, Crosse & Blackwell's marketing emphasized the purity and cleanliness of their bottled sauces—though Heinz capitalized on the idea by selling his products in clear glass bottles.[26] Between them, they revolutionized our use of sauces, making us think of them less as kitchen products and more as something that just appeared on our tables, practically without human effort.

Soyer, following the lead of Carême and predicting the system of Escoffier, said about sauces:

> Sauces in cookery are like the first rudiments of grammar, which consists of certain rules called Syntax, which is the foundation of all languages: these fundamental rules are nine, so has cookery the same number of sauces, which are the foundation of all others; but these, like its prototype the grammar, have two—brown and white, which bear a resemblance to the noun and verb, as they are the first and most easily learnt, and most constantly in use; the others are the adjuncts, pronouns, adverbs, and interjections; upon the proper use of the two principal ones depends the quality of all others, and the proper making of which tends to the enjoyment of the dinner; for to my fancy they are to cookery what the gamut is in the composition of music, as it is by the arrangement of the notes that harmony is produced, so should the ingredients in the sauce be so nicely blended, and that delightful concord should exist, which would equally delight the palate, as a masterpiece of a Mozart or a Rossini should delight the ear; but which, if badly executed, tantalize those nervous organs, affect the whole system, and prove a nuisance instead of a pleasure.[27]

Soyer's words have a lovely metaphoric ring to them but unfortunately do little to advance our understanding of the relationship between our vast collections of possible sauce variations. Escoffier would try to modernize and improve on Soyer's approach. By "modernize," we mean "simplify," because the essence of modernity is simplification—conceptual streamlining.

4

THE FRENCH WERE NOT, OF COURSE, THE ONLY SAUCIERS

At first glance, Italian mother sauces look very familiar; even their spellings reveal their connection to the French hierarchy (though there are a few significant differences).

Besciamella is a white sauce made with pale roux and milk (this is essentially the same as French béchamel, but it may be made with olive oil instead of butter). *Salsa vellutata* is a light-colored sauce made with lightly cooked roux and beef, chicken, or vegetable stock (again, much like the velouté of France). *Salsa spagnola* is a brown sauce made with dark roux cooked in butter or bacon fat, flavored with bay leaves, mirepoix, parsley, and tomato (it's the Italian version of *sauce espagnole*).

The simplest form of *salsa pomodoro* is just tomatoes and mirepoix, but there are hundreds of variations. In French *sauce tomate*, the tomato base is thickened with roux. Italians simply reduce the sauce to the desired consistency, though sometimes pasta is finished in the sauce, and viscosity is adjusted using a bit of the starchy pasta cooking water.

Maionese is a thick emulsion of egg, lemon, olive oil, and vinegar—basically the same as French mayonnaise.

In Spain, sauces are not divided into mother and daughter (or grand and small) sauces, though the primary two—*sofrito* and *picada*—are the basis of many other sauces. The Spanish do have a number of distinct sauce types, however, and they vary somewhat geographically.

Sofrito is both a mixture of aromatic ingredients used as a base for making sauces and a sauce in its own right This garlicky tomato-based sauce is enriched with olive oil and redolent of Iberian herbs (bay leaf, rosemary, and thyme).

Picada, from Catalonia and Valencia, builds on *sofrito* to form other sauces. It is made by pounding fried bread and nuts (usually almonds but also hazelnuts, pine nuts, and/or walnuts), and it is added to other sauces to thicken them. The Catalan "daughter" sauces of *picada* feature garlic, parsley, and saffron. Those from Valencia often show more of the Moorish influence (the Moors occupied the region until the fifteenth century), with added spices such as cinnamon and cumin.

Allioli and *maionese* are closely related culturally and gastronomically. According to some sources, the word "mayonnaise" derives, etymologically, from the Spanish town of Majón, suggesting that the sauce originated there. No one really knows, and its history is hotly contested. In any case, while French aioli might include eggs (making more of a garlic-flavored mayonnaise), the Spanish *allioli* is nothing but oil, garlic, and salt.

Pil-pil is a kind of Basque pan sauce in which olive oil, garlic, and a little hot pepper are emulsified in the gelatin-rich juices that accumulate in the cooking of seafood, often *bacalao* (salt cod) or shrimp.

Catalan *romesco* is a purée of Spanish chiles, thickened—in medieval fashion—with fried bread and ground nuts.[1]

Salsa de tinta, another Basque specialty, includes simmered tomatoes in a mixture of fish stock and local *txakoli* wine, blackened with squid ink. Like *romesco*, it is thickened with fried bread.

Basque *salsa verde* is, like *pil-pil*, garlicky oil combined with the liquid in which the fish was slowly cooked. *Salsa verde* differs from *pil-pil* in that it contains a large amount of minced parsley.

Salsa vizcaina, another Basque specialty, is usually a smooth purée—though sometimes left slightly chunky—of regional chiles (*choriceros*) and tomatoes with olive oil, flavored with garlic, onions, and serrano ham. Aside from the inclusion of ham, *salsa vizcaina* is merely *salsa de tinta* with *choriceros* substituted for squid ink.

Spanish béchamel is the same as the French version, but it's rarely used as a sauce in its own right. It's more often an ingredient in other preparations.

Refrito de ajo is a simple, quick sauce made by deglazing the garlicky oil left in the pan with sherry vinegar, then whisking to emulsify it.

Salsa española is a slightly less fussy take on French *sauce espagnole*. Gallic cooks carefully strain out the spent mirepoix, then thicken the flavored stock with roux, while Spanish sauciers merely purée the aromatics and stir them back in.

Many of the sauces used in Greek dishes are basic cold vinaigrettes, such as *latholémono* (oil and lemon juice) and *lathóxsitho* (oil and vinegar). Greeks do prepare cooked sauces as well, among them the thin, custard-like *avgolemono*, begun by whisking egg (or just egg yolks) together with lemon juice, then tempering with a tiny amount of the hot broth in which the entrée was cooked. More stock is slowly added during continuous whisking until the desired viscosity is obtained. This fragile emulsion cannot be held; it must be served immediately.

Greek béchamel is less fluid than the béchamels of France and Italy. It's almost custard-like, forming the thick layer atop baked dishes like *moussaka* and *pastitsio*. That extra body comes from egg yolks and *kefalotyri*, a hard cheese similar to Italian *romano*. The sauce's delicate perfume comes from freshly grated nutmeg.

Classic *skordaliá* was at one time a pounded emulsion of almonds and garlic in oil and lemon juice. Today, it is often made with much cheaper breadcrumbs or cooked potato instead of almonds.

Sáltsa domátas is the "mother" of all Greek tomato sauces. Tomato purée is slowly cooked with honey, olive oil, onions, and red wine. The basic sauce can then go in a host of directions with the incorporation of assorted herbs, plus cloves and garlic; cinnamon and parsley; cumin and parsley; fresh mint; parsley and bay leaves; or just *rigani* (Greek oregano).

Greeks, like their neighbors throughout the eastern Mediterranean, employ a lot of dips. These flavorful sauces are not served on or under the entrees but appear on the table in separate bowls. This allows diners to adjust their meals to their own tastes.

Further east, one finds that dishes of chickpea hummus are omnipresent, but in Greece *fáva* is the rule. As you might guess, broad fava beans are the legume of choice. Unlike hummus, *fáva* does not include tahini, though yogurt is sometimes added. The Greeks do make hummus from chickpeas (they call it *choúmous*, a name clearly derived from the Arabic, suggesting that the dish did not originate in Greece).

Another dip that exists, in various forms, throughout the region is *tzatziki*. Tangy strained yogurt and refreshing chopped cucumber combine with olive oil, lemon juice, and chopped fresh mint and/or dill to form a dish that balances the attributes of salad and sauce. In fact, leaving out the cucumber, one gets a sauce that accompanies *souvláki* (at least in American diners).

Greek *taramosaláta* is something like a cross between a creamy salmon mousse and a very fishy paté. The seafood, in this case, is the soft salted roe of various fishes (carp, cod, or gray mullet, *Mugil cephalus*), blended into a thick paste with lemon and olive oil. Like *skordaliá*, it was traditionally made with pounded almonds, but today it is likely to be thickened more frugally with bread or cooked potatoes.

The last, but not the least, of these Greek dipping sauces, *melitzano-saláta,* is the scooped-out pulp of smoky grilled eggplant combined with lemon juice, yogurt, garlic, parsley, and olive oil—seasoned with salt, pepper, and rigani (Greek oregano).

Elsewhere in the Middle East, we find some familiar dipping sauces—and some that are quite different. One, a form of hot sauce that enlivens falafel, combines minced garlic, chopped parsley, tomato paste, and *harissa*, thinned with lemon juice and water and simmered to blend all the flavors. *Harissa* is a hot North African condiment containing caraway, chiles, cumin, coriander, garlic, olive oil, and sometimes mint, rose petals (a common ingredient in the Moroccan spice blend *ras al hanout*), and tomatoes. It can be made at home, but most cooks spoon it from a jar or squeeze it out of a convenient tube.

Hummus, unlike the Greek *fáva*, is made of puréed chickpeas ("hummus" is just Arabic for "chickpea"). Virtually all of its ingredients have been farmed in the region for the last ten millennia (one newcomer, lemon, has only been a part of the local diet since the days of the Prophet Muhammad—fourteen centuries ago). Recipes for hummus vary all over the region (Cyprus, Egypt, Iran, Iraq, Israel, Jordan, Lebanon, Palestine, Syria, Turkey, etc.) and have been around since the twelfth century. Everyone in the area, regardless of nationality or religion, eats hummus—even if they disagree about who invented it. This one (minus tahini but including a variety of

Jarred *harissa*, adjunct to many a *tagine* or dish of couscous. *Source:* Gary Allen

flavorings we no longer see in today's recipes for *hummus bi tahini*) is from a medieval text, *Kanz al-Fawa'id fi tanwi' al-Mawa'id*:

Historic Recipe: Purée of Chickpeas with Cinnamon and Ginger

Cook the chickpeas in water, then mash them in a mortar to make a puree. Push the puree through a sieve for wheat, unless it is already fine enough, in which case this step is not necessary. Mix it then with wine vinegar, the pulp of pickled lemons, and cinnamon, pepper, ginger, parsley of the best quality, mint, and rue that have all been chopped and placed on the surface of the serving dish. . . . Finally, pour over [this mixture] a generous amount of oil of good quality.[2]

Other local variations exist, of course. Most garnish their hummus with olive oil (Turks occasionally use olive oil infused with hot chile). Other garnishes include whole chickpeas, fried or toasted pine nuts, olives, fresh herbs, or powdered spices (black pepper, cayenne, cumin, paprika, or sumac). Israelis sometimes either top hummus with favas or replace chickpeas with favas (in which case they call it *ful*) or add meat and/or mushrooms to the chickpea purée. The Syrian fava-based version, *ful medammes*, is (or was)[3] traditionally garnished with Aleppo pepper flakes. Egyptian, Iranian, Iraqi, Lebanese, Syrian, and Turkish hummus can be flavored with cumin. Palestinians are likely to top their hummus with paprika and herbs, such as mint and/or parsley. Jordanians and Turks occasionally replace the tahini with yogurt.

Baba ganoush is hummus's sister sauce. Soft grilled eggplant replaces the chickpea purée. It's the Levantine version of Greek *melitzanosaláta*. Like hummus, it is served throughout the region (Armenia, Egypt, Iraq, Israel, Jordan, Lebanon, Palestine, Syria, and Turkey), again with some local variations. Jordanian *baba ganoush*, *mouttabal*, substitutes salted yogurt for regular yogurt or tahini. Most *baba ganoush* recipes are garnished like hummus, though Iraqis might top it with pomegranate seeds. One Israeli version (*salat ḥatzilim*), however, replaces the traditional tahini or yogurt with—of all things—mayonnaise. Topped with fried onions, it suggests the influence of European emigrants from the Jewish Diaspora. Syrian *baba ganoush* uses neither lemon juice nor tahini nor yogurt; it does feature walnuts, pomegranate molasses, tomato, and sweet red bell pepper and is garnished with pomegranate seeds. An Iranian *baba ganoush*, *mirza ghasemi*, reveals the influence of South Asian cooking; it eliminates tahini and Levantine spices, replacing them with tomatoes and turmeric. Another Iranian variation, *kashke bademjan*, replaces yogurt or tahini with rehydrated *kashk* (pungent central Asian dried yogurt) and ground walnuts. It's flavored with fried garlic, onions, and fresh mint leaves.

Dipping sauces based on olive oil are common through the Levant. Some are as simple as a dish of oil, perhaps sprinkled with some dried herbs. Some slightly more complicated (though "complicated" is a bit of an overstatement) dips might include lemon juice, so they're almost vinaigrettes. One herb (or, rather, type of herb) that can be found mixed with oil on tables anywhere east of the Mediterranean is *za'atar*. The fact that this name is also used for omnipresent herb/spice mixtures merely adds to the confusion, especially since either one could be part of that dipping oil.

> Various mixtures are sometimes marketed as Za'atar (or Zathar). Thyme and Sumac is a common version. Another is: Thyme, Salt, Sumac, and Toasted Sesame. Yet another is: Thyme, Sumac and Summer Savory. I have also seen a melange of Marjoram, Sesame, Sumac, Salt, and Olive Oil. They are probably as unsatisfactory as substitutions for Za'atar as Safflower is for Saffron.
>
> "Za'tar" or "Za'atar" are [also] generic names for a whole group of Middle Eastern herbs from the genera *Origanum*, *Calaminta*, *Thymus* and *Satureja*. In Turkey, *Kekik* is a generic name for a group of herbs that include various Oreganos, Marjorams, Savories, and Thymes.[4]

Either form of *za'atar* might be found as a garnish atop a mixture of olive oil and *labneh* (a form of strained yogurt). The spice blend, along with chopped cilantro and garlic, is a likely addition to dipping oil. Another Middle Eastern spice blend, *dukkah* (an extremely variable mixture of toasted and ground almonds and/or hazelnuts, plus seeds of coriander, cumin, fennel, and sesame—and whatever else a cook might have on hand), might garnish a dish of oil. There are countless other dips, but many of them diverge into forms not liquid enough to be considered sauces.

Moroccans hull and roast the seeds of the argan tree (*Argania spinosa*) and press a nutty aromatic oil, which is used as a dip for bread or a simple sauce for couscous or *tagines*. They also grind toasted almonds in the oil to make *amlou*, a much thicker dip.

Many Far Eastern cuisines feature dipping sauces, usually based on soy sauce, fish sauce, and the like; these will be addressed in detail elsewhere. However, South Asia has a few that should be mentioned here.

Indian *raita*, in its most basic form, is just yogurt infused with cooling mint. Countless variations exist, containing fruits (banana, grape, guava, mango, pineapple, or pomegranate), pulses (sprouted green chickpeas, *boondi* [a sweet made of chickpea flour], or *bhujia sev/matki*[5] and *gram/* chickpea flour), or vegetables (beet, carrot, cucumber, eggplant, onion, potato, pumpkin, spinach, or tomato). South Indian *pachadis* are forms of *raita* incorporating different flavors. Coconut, curry spices, ginger, and mustard are common ingredients.

Chutneys are fruit pickles, some of which are thin enough to be considered sauces. Familiar ones for Indian restaurants include a raw purée of fresh cilantro and mint, green chile, garlic, and ginger suspended in lemon juice and sweetened water; and *imli*, a cooked sauce of moistened tamarind (*Tamarindus indica*) pulp with spices (cumin, fennel, garlic, ginger, *hing*,[6] and the blend garam masala[7]) in enough sugar water to provide the correct dipping viscosity. Slightly less familiar are *saunth* (another cooked tamarind sauce, this time with cumin, hot chile, garam masala, and powdered ginger, plus *kala namak*[8] and jaggery[9]) and *tamatar kasundi* (a sweet-sour and spicy Bengali chutney based on tomatoes, seasoned with brown mustard seeds, brown sugar, fresh chiles and chile powder, cumin, garlic, ginger, oil, turmeric, and vinegar).

In Southeast Asia, a table that is not set with a bowl of dipping sauce is almost unthinkable. Many derive their umami from fermented seafood. Burmese, Indonesian, and Thai cooks lace their sauces with salty shrimp paste. For the Vietnamese the omnipresent fish sauce (*nuóc mám*) becomes *nuóc chám*—or *nam chim kai* for the Thais—when combined with garlic, minced hot chile, lime juice, sugar, and vinegar. The same sauce, in Cambodia, is called *tirk trey chu p'em* and might be garnished with chopped peanuts. Vietnamese *nuóc mám me*—or Cambodian *tirk umpel*—adds tamarind paste to the basic recipe. Adding ginger to *nuóc chám* yields *nuóc mám gung* (*tirk khngay* in Cambodia). A cooked version of *nuóc chám*, with lemongrass and onion, is Burmese *ngan pya ye chet*.

Vietnamese diners love to wrap foods in leaves (cool, crisp lettuce, for example), spreading a bit of one of their dips and adding a handful of fresh herbs for a casual meal. Koreans have a similar approach; they call their handheld wraps *ssam*. The leaves are more varied, however, with seasonal choices like bean leaves, cabbage, lettuce, pumpkin leaves, and seaweed (*miyeok-wakame* or dried *gim-nori* in Japanese). They spread the leaves with *ssamjang*, literally "sauce for wrapped food." These thick sauces are made with the usual Korean ingredients—dark sesame oil, *doenjang* (fermented soybean paste), *gochujang* (hot, sweet fermented chile paste), onion, garlic, and scallion—and sometimes sweetened with brown sugar.

Indonesian sauces, generically called *sambals*, are complex compositions of sweet, sour, hot, and umami. Many begin with shrimp paste (*belachan*), tamarind paste, and hot chiles, pounded together to form a dark and savory paste called *sambal oelek*. That and *sambal nasi goreng*—thick, sweet soy sauce (*kecap manis*), shallot, garlic, tamarind and shrimp pastes, and chiles—are mass produced by a Dutch company, Conimex, reflecting more than four centuries of trade between the two distant lands.

These Southeast Asian sauces are clearly related to each other, and many of them reveal the influence of Chinese methods. Their cooks don't seem to have been concerned with trying to create taxonomies of mother and daughter sauces, as the French were.

Today, the foundation of most Chinese sauces is soybeans, fermented with salt in various ways.[10] *Háoyóu* (oyster sauce) is produced by long simmering of raw oysters, straining out the spent oysters, and then adding more. The process is repeated until the desired viscosity and intensity of umami are achieved (though most commercial sauces get the same result, more quickly, by mixing in soy sauce and starch).

Curiously, oyster sauce has an origin story similar to that of other sauces: A cook—Li Jinshang, founder of Lee Kum Lee, still a major producer of Chinese sauces—was, as the story goes, cooking oysters and forgot about them until the liquid had almost boiled away. Noticing its rich aroma, he tasted the resulting substance, and the rest is history. Unfortunately, while entertaining, the same sort of questionable history recounts the discovery of Worcestershire sauce and, for that matter, the origins of roast pork, as described in Charles Lamb's humorous essay, in which a farmer discovered a delicious smell after his pig was lost when the barn burned down (and, from then on, burned a barn every time he wanted roast pork)!

Typical oyster sauce. *Source:* Gary Allen

Li Jinshang's company has grown considerably since 1888. Its product line, intended for home and restaurant kitchens, includes (in addition to five oyster sauces) a dozen soy sauces, a couple of XO sauces, a large assortment of ready-made sauces and dipping sauces, and an entire range of hot sauces, including several variations on *sriracha*. Many of these products are fermented—in other words, they are classically Chinese.

XO sauces are a century newer than oyster sauce. Originally from Hong Kong, they are now made in several places. Dried scallops, shrimps, ham, the salted roe of *mentaiko* (pollock, *Pollachius* spp.), tiny anchovies (called *shirasu*), and/or other salted and dried fish provide a massive jolt of umami, while garlic and onion add additional savoriness, and chile pepper provides the final kick. XO sauce is used both in Cantonese cooking and as a condiment at table.

In the New World, several different sauce traditions are in effect. Looking at the oldest, first, we find the *salsas*. They were made from Mexico through Central America and in parts of South America. Today, they are enjoyed worldwide. These are suspensions of various vegetable or fruit purées—commonly chiles and tomatoes—in acidic fruit juices. They may be cooked or raw but are generally produced in a mortar and pestle made of coarse-textured lava rock, called a *molcajete*. The same device is used to make guacamole, a

Freshly made guacamole in a *molcajete*. *Source:* Gary Allen

smooth or lumpy mash of avocados that may or may not be garnished with minced hot chiles (typically jalapeños or serranos), chopped tomato, onion, garlic, or cilantro and is often moistened with lime juice.

Mexican moles and *pipians* are cooked sauces, the latter thickened with pumpkin seeds, much like the ground nuts of Spanish *picadas* from which they're descended. Spanish *romesco* is another descendant of *picadas*.[11] Pre-Columbian Mexicans already made moles, but the complex spicing they have now reflects the influence of the Moors on medieval Spanish cooking (*mole poblano*, for example, incorporates many ingredients that hadn't existed in the New World before the Spanish arrived: almonds, cinnamon, cloves, coriander seeds, raisins, and sesame seeds). Suspensions of pounded herbs in oil and/or citrus juice or vinegar—like Argentinian *chimichurri*—rival *salsas*, but more as a condiment, at table, than as a dipping sauce.

Perhaps the biggest influence on the modern world's use of sauces comes from North America. A trip down the condiment aisle of any American grocery store can be overwhelming. Since the nineteenth century, mass marketing of industrially produced sauces has nearly unified the eating habits of the planet. Ketchup can be found everywhere—from the curry-flavored version that tops hot dogs in Berlin to the slightly less vinegary one sold in Australia as "tomato sauce." American mustards—while not as prestigious as those from Dijon or Düsseldorf—spread bright yellow cheer around the globe. Hot sauces, barbecue sauces, dips, marinades, salad dressings, and *salsas*, not to mention dessert toppings like caramel, hot fudge, and—may the world forgive us—marshmallow fluff, abound.

The sheer number and variety of all these condiments, dips, and sauces is mind boggling, but we believe there is a way to understand how they are made and how they connect to or differ from each other.

5

THE MODERN WORLD
OF COOKING BEGINS

If the Enlightenment created an environment in which a taste for taxonomic order could flourish, imagine what it was like in the first quarter of the twentieth century. World War I had just wiped out the romantic excesses of the fin de siècle and ushered in a newly recognizable modern world. This was a world in which new media allowed rapid communication across vast distances. A world in which (in Germany's Bauhaus, for example) architects and designers were experimenting with a spare aesthetic that abandoned frivolous decoration in favor of disciplined order. A world in which mass production, à la Henry Ford's assembly line, was making individually produced items seem quaintly obsolete. A world in which efficiency, inspired by scientific thinking, was the new watchword. In that intellectual milieu, Auguste Escoffier (1846–1935) refined the taxonomy attempted by Antoine Carême.

Escoffier began his kitchen apprenticeship at the age of thirteen. By eighteen, he had already been promoted to saucier at Le Petit Moulon Rouge in Paris. In 1866, he served, briefly, in the French military at the front in the Franco-Prussian War—and, like Alexis Soyer, he learned the value of efficiency in preparing food (albeit at a more spartan level than he had done in Paris) for large numbers of diners. At age thirty, he opened his own restaurant, Le Faisan Doré, in Cannes. Eight years later, he began his association with César Ritz, and from then on their careers were synonymous with the golden age of hotel restaurants. It was the sort of fast-paced work environment that depended on the organizational skills he brought to the proverbial table.

Escoffier published four editions of his *Guide culinaire*—in which he laid out his system of mother sauces—between 1903 and 1921. He later wrote, "I didn't want the *Guide* to be a luxurious work of art or a curiosity that would be relegated to library shelves. I wanted it to be a work tool more than a book, a constant companion that chefs would always keep at their side. . . . I cannot pretend that it is exhaustive. Even if it were finished today, it would be out-of-date tomorrow, because progress never stops."[1]

Escoffier designed his system to simplify the workings of a professional kitchen, but his culinary ideas reached a much larger audience, in part because of improvements in communication, much as the printing press had enabled the diffusion of knowledge in the sixteenth century. His employees also spread the word. According to Priscilla Parkhurst Ferguson, "He boasted that the two thousand or so chefs that he had trained in his kitchens in Paris and in London were scattered all over the globe where their culinary progeny practiced what the master preached."[2]

Escoffier's family tree of basic sauces allowed the sauciers in his *brigade de cuisine* (another of his organizational inventions, one that reflected his experience of military hierarchies during the war years) to simply add ingredients to one of the "mother" sauces already on hand. This system permitted them to make new "daughter" sauces without needing to start each sauce from scratch. Escoffier was still producing haute cuisine in his luxurious hotel restaurants, but, somewhere in the background, Henry Ford's practicality was at work in the kitchen.

Escoffier took Carême's basic idea but tweaked it, adding categories as needed and demoting one. He perfected the *sauce allemande* (German sauce) but didn't consider it one of the mother sauces. He wrote, "Allemande Sauce or thickened Velouté is not, strictly speaking, a basic sauce. However, it is so often resorted to in the preparation of other sauces that I think it necessary to give it after the Veloutés, from which it is derived."[3]

His variation on velouté, with elements of hollandaise, is enriched with egg yolks, additional white stock, and mushroom liquor. When World War I began—and all things German lost some of their cachet—he gave the first of his daughter sauces a new name: *sauce blonde*. (Remember freedom fries?

We were not the first to indulge in such nationalistic foolishness.) Now that the hostilities are over, it's better known as *sauce parisienne*.

LES FONDS: THE MOTHER SAUCES

Béchamel is a milk-based sauce, thickened with a white roux, seasoned with salt, and flavored as needed. In America, it is simply called "white sauce."

Historic Recipe: Béchamel

This sauce is made from equal parts butter and flour by weight, which combine to make a white roux. Then milk and salt are added, along with other spices depending on the recipe. Here is a basic béchamel recipe:

Ingredients

5 Tbsp.	butter
4 Tbsp.	flour
4 cups	milk (can be adjusted for thickness)
2 Tbsp.	salt
to taste	pepper or nutmeg

Method

1. Heat the milk in a saucepan. While it is warming, melt the butter in another pan.
2. Add the flour and stir to create a white roux. Slowly add the heated milk in increments to the roux, whisking all the while. When the desired thickness and smoothness is achieved, bring the mix to a boil.
3. Reduce the heat and stir frequently for 3 to 5 more minutes.
4. Add salt and pepper to taste.[4]

Escoffier's version was considerably richer. He carefully cooked lean veal and onions in butter, without browning them, and simmered them in the béchamel along with a sprig of thyme. The sauce was of course strained before use. The only time he made the sauce *without* veal was during Lent.

Velouté is a light stock-based sauce, thickened with a pale roux or—in some modern versions—a liaison (a mixture of egg yolks and cream). Like béchamel, velouté starts with a roux. The main difference between the two sauces is that velouté uses white stock as a liquid, while béchamel calls for milk.

Historic Recipe: Velouté

Ingredients

2 cups	white stock (Velouté is traditionally made with veal stock. However, chicken or fish stock will do.)
3 Tbsp.	butter
3 Tbsp.	flour
to taste	salt and pepper

Method

1. Melt down the butter until it is frothy. Add the flour and stir frequently to create a roux. Velouté is not as white as Béchamel, so allow the roux to cook until it develops a golden color.
2. Whisk in the stock in half-cup increments until the mixture is smooth.
3. Then add the desired amount of salt and pepper.
4. Bring the sauce to a boil, then reduce the heat and let it simmer for around 20 minutes.[5]

As velouté was an essential element of Escoffier's family of mother sauces, he was very particular about its preparation: "I am not partial to garnishing Velouté sauce with carrots, an onion with a clove stuck into it, and an herb bunch, as many do. The stock should be sufficiently fragrant itself, without requiring the addition of anything beyond the usual condiments."[6] He liked the flavor imparted by mushroom peelings but used them only in preparing his stock to avoid discoloring the delicate sauce.

Espagnole is a fortified brown veal-stock sauce, thickened with a brown roux.

Historic Recipe: Espagnole

Ingredients

2 lb.	mirepoix
8 oz.	clarified butter
8 oz.	flour
5 qt.	brown stock

8 oz.	tomato purée
1	bay leaf
½ tsp.	thyme
¼ tsp.	peppercorns
8	parsley stems

Method

1. Sauté mirepoix in butter until well browned.
2. Add flour and cook to make a brown roux.
3. Add the stock and tomato purée. Stir to break up any lumps of roux. Bring to a boil and then immediately reduce to a simmer.
4. Add the sachet. Simmer for about 1.5 hours to reduce. Skim the surface periodically.
5. Strain through a china cap with cheesecloth. Season to taste.[7]

Escoffier's version takes much longer—up to two days longer—with additional brown stock added to make up for losses due to evaporation. When the sauce is finished, it can be made into demi-glace by combining equal parts of sauce and brown stock, reduced yet again, then fortified with "excellent sherry. 'Demi-Glace' . . . is the base of all the smaller brown sauces."[8]

Hollandaise is a cooked emulsion of egg yolk, butter, and lemon or vinegar.

Historic Recipe: Hollandaise

Ingredients

½ fl. oz.	white vinegar
½ fl. oz.	water
2	egg yolks
12 oz.	clarified butter (heated to 52°C/125°F)
to taste	lemon juice
to taste	cayenne pepper

Method

1. Combine yolks, water, and vinegar.
2. Cook quickly over a double boiler until yolks are lighter in color and a ribbon consistency, then remove from heat.
3. Heat clarified butter to 52°C/125°F.

4. Slowly add butter to yolks, whisking constantly. Add a few drops of lemon juice if sauce seems too thick.
5. Season to taste with salt, cayenne and lemon juice.
6. Hot hold at 52°C/125°F for 1.5 hours maximum.[9]

Escoffier's version is at once simpler and more elegant—and richer. It uses a greater proportion of egg yolks and, instead of cayenne, mignonette pepper (the highest-quality white pepper). To ensure a perfect texture, the finished sauce is pushed through a fine sieve.

Sauce tomate is, as one would expect, tomato based—but, as with the tomato sauce of Soyer, it does not resemble any tomato sauce (marinara or puttanesca) one might find in a typical Italian red sauce joint. Like most of Escoffier's sauce recipes, it features both flour and butter. To quote Mark Twain, completely out of context, "It is un-American. It is un-English. It is *French!*"

Historic Recipe: Tomate

Ingredients

5 oz.	salted breast of pork, rather fat
6 oz.	carrots, cut into cubes
6 oz.	onions, cut into cubes
1	bay leaf
1	small sprig thyme
5 oz.	flour
2 oz.	butter
½ oz.	salt
1 oz.	sugar
pinch	pepper
10 lbs.	raw tomatoes (or 4 qts. of same, mashed)
2 qts.	white stock

Method

1. Fry the pork with the butter in a tall, thick-bottomed saucepan. When the pork is nearly melted, add the carrots, onions and aromatics.
2. Cook and stir the vegetables, then add the flour, which should be allowed to cook until it begins to brown.
3. Now put in the tomatoes and white stock, mix the whole mixture well, and set to boil on an open fire.

4. At this point add the seasoning and a crushed clove of garlic, cover the saucepan, and place in a moderate oven, where it may cook for 1.5 hours.
5. At the end of this time the sauce should be passed through a sieve or tammy, and it should boil while being stirred.
6. Finally, pour it into a tureen, and butter its surface to avoid the formation of a skin.[10]

This is, essentially, Escoffier's version of *sauce tomate*. The only difference is that Escoffier sometimes used canned tomatoes. Don't be shocked; the use of canned tomatoes was pioneered in Escoffier's kitchens. He explained,

> Crushed tomato appeared on the market around 1892. But the idea of producing it came in 1874–75, when I was chef at Le Petit Moulin Rouge. . . . This purée could only be used for tomato sauce. I thought the taste could be improved, and carried out tests that were entirely satisfactory. I . . . spoke of it to several manufacturers, but no one was interested in the idea. Fifteen years later I was able to convince a fruit and vegetable canning factory to produce 2,000 cans of crushed tomato that were immediately sent to the Savoy. They were very much appreciated, and canned tomato sauce was launched. . . . Later, the rate of production increased . . . spreading to Italy and America. Today millions of cans of tomato sauce are sold.[11]

Who could imagine that the canned tomato sauce that is standard in pizza joints and the most ordinary red sauce restaurants was the brainchild of the master of elegant, white-tablecloth restaurants more than a century ago?

Julia Child was once asked about the legacy of Escoffier, given the changes wrought by nouvelle cuisine and the increasing internationalization of modern cooking. She replied, "I think when you read Escoffier's introductions . . . you see he had very contemporary ideas. When he was writing about sauces like *espagnole* and *demi-glace*, he said that there would probably be simpler ways of doing things in the future. I think his idea was that cuisine has to adapt to the times."[12]

Escoffier's system was based on just a few mother sauces and a presumably infinite number of daughter sauces created by adding garnishes or seasonings to the basic mother sauces. Today's cooks see sauces somewhat differently—and Escoffier would probably appreciate an approach that is, at once, more inclusive and systematic than was required a century ago.

Perhaps, instead of just mothers and daughters, we should think of sauces as part of large extended families, both in the sense of the usual collection of aunts, uncles, nieces, nephews, and numerous grandparents and great-grandparents endlessly receding into history and in the way that biologists view taxonomies. A biological family is defined by its evolution from a common ancestor as well as by its particular assemblage of physical charac-teristics. It might be more constructive—and instructive—for us to consider sauces in their familial contexts.

II

O BRAVE NEW WORLD, THAT HAS SUCH SAUCES IN IT!

6

TIME FOR A CHANGE

As we have seen, Auguste Escoffier's system of mother and daughter sauces became the standard for understanding the otherwise chaotic nature of, and connections between, sauces.

However, when we look at the hierarchy of sauces created by Escoffier (and Antoine Carême before him), a few drawbacks present themselves. First, we notice that almost all his mother sauces share a common feature: they are thickened with flour. Hollandaise is the only exception. A larger issue is that very few people today use sauces like those (even classically trained French chefs employ a range of sauces that Escoffier could never have imagined). Today's kitchens are much more cosmopolitan than those of a century ago.

It is true that French chefs have always explored the cuisines of other cultures, but they generally adopted one ingredient or another, which they then employed in a classically French manner. Something labeled "Florentine" would not be recognizable to a citizen of Firenze; it would merely be a French dish that contains spinach. A dish served à la japonaise would seem even more bizarre in Tokyo (since it could be a salad containing artichokes, mussels, potatoes, and/or truffles). The descriptor à la japonaise is also applied to a bombe of peach ice cream, though the only remotely Japanese thing about the latter is its tea-scented filling.

Another issue involved in the naming of sauces adds a complication. Like the common names for plants and animals—which vary from place to place and from time to time—we would prefer a more consistent system of nomenclature to make sense of them. In biology, a system of taxonomy was created, using Latin binomials, to try to minimize confusion. That will be impossible for sauces, but we can at least try to acknowledge the problem and point out the differences between similar names—while revealing the shared characteristics of related sauces. Take, for example, the following recipe, from 1861, by Mrs. Beeton:

Historic Recipe: Remoulade, or French Salad-Dressing

Ingredients

4	eggs
½ Tbsp.	made mustard
to taste	salt and cayenne
3 Tbsp.	olive oil
1 Tbsp.	tarragon or plain vinegar

Method

1. Boil 3 eggs quite hard for about ¼ hour, put them into cold water, and let them remain in it for a few minutes; strip off the shells, put the yolks in a mortar, and pound them very smoothly; add to them, very gradually, the mustard, seasoning, and vinegar, keeping all well stirred and rubbed down with the back of a wooden spoon.
2. Put in the oil drop by drop, and when this is thoroughly mixed with the other ingredients, add the yolk of a raw egg, and stir well, when it will be ready for use.
3. This sauce should not be curdled; and to prevent this, the only way is to mix a little of everything at a time, and not to cease stirring.
4. The quantities of oil and vinegar may be increased or diminished according to taste, as many persons would prefer a smaller proportion of the former ingredient.[1]

Her recipe does not resemble any rémoulade—or, for that matter, any French salad dressing—we would recognize today. Compare, for example, this recipe of Escoffier's from 1903:

Historic Recipe: 130 Sauce Remoulade

To one pint of Mayonnaise (126) add one large tablespoon of prepared mustard, another of gherkins, and yet another of chopped and pressed out capers, one tablespoon of fine herbs, parsley, chervil, and tarragon, all chopped and mixed, and a teaspoon of anchovy *essence* or anchovy paste.[2]

Escoffier's sauce not only looks like ours but also builds on preexisting sauces more efficiently, much as we would today. Forty years (and a taste for modernity) made all the difference.

Today's chefs—and many home cooks—think nothing of creating entirely new sauces that might include chile pastes (like Korean *gochujang* or Peruvian *ají amarillo*) or fish sauces (like Vietnamese *pla ra* or British anchovy essence). We thicken our sauces not just with reduced cream or starchy roux but also with ground nuts and seeds, or we purée exotic fruits and vegetables. We routinely incorporate ingredients and techniques—from every far-flung corner of the world, and every culture and every time period—in ways never imagined by classically trained French chefs.

Our palates are not just more eclectic. We also have a desire for authenticity in our food (even if we're not entirely certain what "authentic" really means). We don't want a French dish that merely nods at another culture's culinary traditions; we want the real thing.

But Escoffier's list of mother sauces seems inadequate for another reason. We live in a more technological world, one in which we expect at least the trappings of a scientific approach. Escoffier's system reflects the thinking of a different century, a different millennium. We may not always be logical in our thinking about sauces, but we expect an approach that is more substantial than four starches and one lonely emulsion.

While Escoffier created a number of bottled sauces for use in the home, his system isn't flexible enough to address our broadened tastes. Escoffier, like Carême before him, had an architect's desire to control the experience of his clients. That kind of ego seems foolishly out of place when we think nothing of having BBQ sauce, honey-mustard sauce, ketchup, piri piri, a couple of soy sauces, *sriracha*, Tabasco, or Worcestershire on our tables— maybe at the same time.

Alice May Brock, of *Alice's Restaurant* fame, once said, "Tomatoes and oregano make it Italian; wine and tarragon make it French. Sour cream makes it Russian; lemon and cinnamon make it Greek. Soy sauce makes it Chinese; garlic makes it good." We've gone beyond such one-size-fits-all notions about food and cooking (let alone the arrogance implied in reducing entire "ethnic"[3] cuisines to just a few ingredients or flavors). We know that cuisines have evolved and continue to evolve in response to a host of different conditions: immigration, wars, and economic and environmental changes. Even a subject as narrow as "sauces" can reflect all those things. This makes any attempt to make sense of it all both difficult and fascinating. How, for example, would Escoffier's taxonomy categorize the creations of molecular gastronomy?

Clearly a completely different approach is required. It must be flexible enough to incorporate any sauce, from any part of the world that now exists, has ever existed, or is ever likely to exist. It must be able to address any sauce, regardless of the unusualness of its ingredients. It must be logical and able to function without having to build on historical sauce precedents—yet able to seamlessly accommodate any of those preexisting sauces. While we're at it, we should take a look at the way different cultures have adopted and adapted sauces from other places—or, in some cases, created them independently of one another utilizing similar techniques or methodologies.

In 1991, cookbook author James Peterson took on the challenge. His book, *Sauces: Classical and Contemporary Sauce Making*, is monumental in scope. Like Raymond Sokolov, he worked from the sauce maker's perspective, but he went beyond Sokolov's classical French sauces to incorporate the wider range of sauces prepared by today's cooks. Unfortunately—at least as regards our preference for "simpler is better"—his taxonomy required at least seventeen primary categories.

There may be other ways to accomplish the goal of devising a comprehensive taxonomy, but the simplest that comes to mind is based on the physical structures of the sauces. To that end, let us consider five new mother sauce categories (plus a hybrid category, "composites," for sauces that merge characteristics of two or more of the five primaries).

Appropriately enough, the first of the solutions to our self-imposed task is in fact . . . solutions.

7

SOLUTIONS

A solution is the simplest form of sauce. It consists of either single molecules or their constituent ions, distributed evenly throughout a solvent. Ions are molecules that have broken into their elemental parts, like the sodium and chlorine atoms that make up salt. When one heats a liquid (solvent) or stirs it vigorously, dissolvable material (solute) is broken into tinier and tinier bits. Eventually, those bits reach the point at which the mere movement of the solvent's molecules[1] is enough to keep the bits of solute from joining into clumps large enough for the force of gravity to overcome the combination of molecular motion and surface tension and cause them to settle out of solution.

Transparency provides an easy way to recognize a solution. If any particles larger than single molecules are floating around in a liquid, they tend to scatter the light as it's transmitted, so the liquid appears cloudy, translucent, or even opaque. If it's clear, it's probably a solution.

Perhaps the simplest sauce is one found in nature: honey. Bees collect nectar from flowers and fan it with their wings to reduce it by evaporation. We do the same thing, using heat, to make maple syrup or to produce concentrated *glace de viande* from meat stock (a mixture of a soluble protein and collagen, plus flavoring and coloring compounds, created by Maillard reactions that occur when mirepoix, proteins, and fat are heated).

Some common methods for the production of flavorful solutions are simple dissolving, infusion and maceration, steeping and simmering, filtration, distillation, and fermentation.

The simplest solutions are brines and syrups made by stirring the solute into a solvent (though adding heat can speed the process) or by reducing a liquid that already contains the solute. In South America, the juice of sugar cane is combined with orange zest, then reduced to a syrup (*chancaca*) that serves as a topping for desserts. Sri Lankans tap toddy fishtail palms (*Caryota urens*), then boil the sap into a syrup called *kithul peni*. It's employed much as we use honey and maple syrup. If reduced further, it becomes the sticky brown sugar known as jaggery (hence the tree's local name, "jaggery palm")—unless it's fermented into palm wine first. Other syrups in common use are derived from the sap of agave, birches, and sorghum.

Historic Recipe: Royal Sauce[2]

Take a terra cotta pot of new earth [a new pot] and put inside it two pounds of good sugar, and four glassfuls of strong white vinegar, and twelve whole cloves, and a piece of good cinnamon stick cut very finely. Then put it to the fire over the coals and make it to boil so much that should thicken it and skim it well, and watch that it does not get too thick, and a small amount of ground nutmeg shall be good.[3]

Bartolomeo Scappi's "Royal Sauce" was clearly a sweet-sour solution of sugar and white vinegar, thickened only by reduction.

Vincotto is heavily reduced sweet must;[4] it has been made in much the same way since ancient times. The ancient Greeks had a word for it, *itepsima* (modern Greeks call it *petimezi*), while the Romans called it *defrutum* or *caroenum*, depending on how sweet (how reduced) it was. These Roman syrups were often flavored with spices, unlike *sapa*, which was unflavored reduced must. *Pekmez* is a modern Turkish version (note the similarity with *petimezi*), made from grapes, mulberries, or even sugar beets. It is sweeter than *nar ekşisi* (Turkish pomegranate "molasses"), which appears in dishes from all over the eastern Mediterranean region. Reduced fruit juices are sometimes used as is as sauces or combined with other liquids to make more complex sauces. *Vincotto* can be mixed with wine vinegar and aged to produce something akin to balsamic vinegar.

Infusing is merely soaking some material (usually the leaves or flowers of an herb or other plant) in a hot liquid. Teas and tisanes are typical infusions. Maceration is just like infusion but with larger particles sitting in a cold liquid. One method for making raspberry vinegar, for example, is to soak berries in vinegar, then filter out the solids and dissolve some sugar to bring out the berries' flavor. *Vincotto*-based surrogates for balsamic vinegar may be flavored with any number of fruits; citrus, figs, and berries are common. *Oxymel* (a mixture of honey and vinegar) was once used to preserve fruits, such as grapes, pears, and quinces, and functioned as a sauce when serving them.

In some cases, the solution is just a by-product—the solids, infused with the flavor of the solvent, are the goal. Some soy sauces are merely the remnants of the production of seasoning pastes. Such fermented pastes, like the *tu'o'ng* of Vietnam and Chinese *doubanjiang* (salted and ground broad beans, soybeans, chiles), are the basis of many Asian sauces. Korean *ssamjang* is a mixture of two other pastes, *doenjang* (salted soy) and *gochujang* (hot chiles, glutinous rice, fermented soybeans, and salt), plus brown sugar, onions, scallions, garlic, and sesame oil. It accompanies grilled meats, just as ketchup and mustard appear at an American cookout.

Steeping is another word for infusing. It differs from simmering in that hot solvent is poured over the potential solute, whereas in simmering, long, slow cooking at sub-boiling temperatures gradually dissolves components that would otherwise be insoluble. The collagen in bones and tough meats, for example, is dissolved by simmering to make stock. All of Auguste Escoffier's mother sauces, other than hollandaise, begin with stock. He said, "Stock is everything in cooking, at least in French cooking. Without it, nothing can be done. If one's stock is good, what remains of the work is easy; if, on the other hand, it is bad or merely mediocre, it is quite hopeless to expect anything approaching a satisfactory result."[5] If the stock (made from beef and especially veal bones, which are incompletely calcified and so are much richer in soluble collagen) is reduced even further, it becomes gelatin-rich demi-glace, which can be used to thicken and enrich transparent sauces. Classic *sauce bordelaise*, for example, employs reduced red Bordeaux wine, plus melted demi-glace and bits of beef marrow, to enhance grilled steaks.

A macerated or infused liquid is often filtered to produce a clear solution. Filtration involves passing a liquid containing some solids (generally ground or chopped) through a material that allows the flavored liquid to pass but not the solids. Coffee is commonly brewed and filtered.

Why mention a beverage that isn't, itself, a sauce? Because it's an ingredient in several sweet dessert sauces. Less obviously, the brew appears in savory sauces, such as southern red-eye gravy and Portuguese *bife à café* (steak in coffee sauce that combines milky coffee with bay leaf, garlic, pepper, red wine, and butter, thickened with corn starch). Less surprisingly, coffee is an ingredient in many barbecue sauces—less surprisingly because practically anything can find, and has found, its way into recipes for barbecue.

Distillation first heats a liquid, converting it to a vapor, then cools the resulting gas to condense its components. Fractional distillation involves the use of heat to separate a mixture of solutions into their individual solutions, each of which boils at a different temperature. Alcohol boils at a lower temperature than water, making it possible to increase the concentration of alcohol in a fermented liquid. Wine, which is a complex solution of alcohol, water, and dozens of flavoring compounds, can be distilled to make brandy, which is then aged in oak barrels that infuse it with new flavors. The distillation of wine is not perfect (which would yield only ethyl alcohol), because some flavoring compounds are volatile at temperatures close to that of alcohol—one reason why brandy, whiskey, and tequila don't taste like vodka. By the way, alcohol freezes at a much lower temperature than water does, so potent apple jack can be "distilled" by freezing the water component of hard cider and pouring off the higher-proof liquid that remains.

Wines made from rice instead of fruit (technically, beers without carbonation) are essential to the cooking of several Asian regions.

The Japanese have mirin, which is basically a type of seasoned cooking sake with reduced alcohol and elevated sugar. One mirin-based sauce, *nikiri mirin*, is ten parts soy sauce, two parts dashi (an umami-rich stock made from dried skipjack flakes and kombu seaweed),[6] and one part each of mirin and sake. A shortcut version uses only four parts tamari to one of mirin. Either way, it is reduced (*ni-kiru* is Japanese for "boil down") to form a glaze applied to fish that's about to be served. A similar sauce, *nitsume*, substitutes a reduced gelatinous broth made from conger eel for the dashi and sugar for the sake. It is only used on types of sushi that incorporate cooked seafood, such as eel, octopus, or shrimp.

Japanese glazed dishes, known as *teriyaki*, are coated with a reduced mixture of mirin (or sake), plus soy sauce and sugar. In the United States, ready-made bottles of teriyaki sauce are sold—though the Japanese don't consider teriyaki a sauce, and even if they did, they certainly wouldn't include sesame oil and garlic in its formulation.

Mirin is also the base for *ponzu* dipping sauce. It's simmered with rice vinegar and the basic ingredients for dashi—kombu seaweed and flakes of *katsuobushi* (fermented, dried, and smoked skipjack tuna, *Katsuwonus pelamis*)—then soured with citrus juice. That juice could come from any of the following citrus fruits: lemon; *daidai* or citrus and *daidai*; *kabosu*, *C. sphaerocarpa*; *sudachi*, *C. sudachi*; or *yuzu*, *C. junos*.

The best-known Chinese wine is *huangjiu*, made in Shaoxing in Zhen-jiang province. It comes in three basic forms: *yuanhong*, *jiafan*, and *shan-niang*, with *yuanhong* being the driest and *shanniang* the sweetest. All are long aged in earthenware jars and have a nutty, sherry-like taste. *Huangjiu* is usually seen in the West as Shaoxing rice cooking wine, which—like the

Shaoxing rice (cooking) wine. *Source:* Gary Allen

CHAPTER 7

so-called cooking wines we find in our grocery stores—has salt added to dis-
courage people from drinking it (and to comply with laws that control sales
of alcoholic beverages). Drunken chicken, a classic Shaoxing dish, is made
by poaching the bird with ginger and scallion, then soaking it overnight
in the local rice wine. It's cut up and served cold with a sauce made of the
poaching and marinating liquids.

Korean rice wine, *cheongju* or *mirim*, is similar to Japanese mirin in that
it has some residual sweetness (in some cases, sugar or corn syrup is added).
Either one can be used in Korean dishes. *Mihyang* marinade, which is available ready-made, is *cheongju* and vinegar, sweetened with sugar or corn
syrup. It's usually employed to flavor pork dishes. Koreans also sweeten
their dishes with plum syrup (*maesil cheong*), made by aging green plums in
sugar. The hygroscopic sugar gradually draws moisture and flavorings from
the fruit, which is then strained for use.

Perhaps the most unexpected source of solutions—but most globally
widespread—is fermentation. We're talking about sauces, not just alcohol
(even if alcohol is sometimes referred to, colloquially, as "the sauce"). Alcohol, in various forms, is a component of many sauces, such as Scottish whiskey sauce (flamed whiskey, reduced cream, salt, and pepper) or Italian *penne
alla vodka* (also based on heavy cream but colored by tomato purée with
onions and garlic that have been sautéed in butter). Wines (red, white, Ma-
deira, sherry), in combination with other ingredients, provide the foundation
of the sauces for countless classic dishes—from *boeuf bourguignon* to *coq au
vin*—though red barbera wine is, all by itself, a sauce for pasta in Piemonte.

Let's focus, instead, on nonalcoholic fermentation and its products.
When minute organisms (mostly yeasts, molds, and bacteria) digest solid
nutrients in a liquid environment, they extract their soluble components
and, at the same time, create many new compounds that were not present in the original solids. Brine is often the liquid employed because it is
inhospitable to dangerous bacteria but encourages the growth of desirable
species. The ancient Romans' *garum* and soy sauce are classic brine-based
fermented solutions (that also employ enzymatic hydrolysis). Vinegar is
another familiar example, though it's fermented without salt.

Before we dive into any of these solutions, let's examine a key set of
ingredients that many sauces have in common: a base mixture of aromatic
vegetables. They are generally cooked slowly in fat until they have browned

and developed complex flavors through caramelization and/or Maillard reactions. A liquid is added to them to extract as much soluble flavor and color as possible. The solids are strained out, having added depth of flavor and aroma in solution. Cuisines that utilize aromatics in this way tend not to employ sauces made from brined soluble proteins (such as soy sauce or the fish sauces of Southeast Asia). Generally, aromatics are not employed there because the fermented sauces provide more than enough umami and other flavors on their own.

In French cooking, the aromatic of choice is mirepoix: two parts onion and one part each of carrots and celery. White mirepoix substitutes leeks for the carrots when a light-colored sauce is desired. In Cajun recipes, the aromatic base is called "trinity": it's still mirepoix but substitutes green pepper for the carrots. *Battuto* or *sofritto* (also known as "holy trinity") is the Italian take on mirepoix, adding garlic and sometimes cured pork products—pancetta or prosciutto. The Spanish version, *sofrito*, replaces the green peppers with red and the carrots with tomatoes—and Catalonian *sofrito* adds garlic. Filipinos have adopted a form of *sofrito* that is almost identical to that of Spain, but they call it *ginisá*. Puerto Rican *sofrito* is based on several sweet peppers (*ajices dulces, cubanelles*, red bell peppers), plus cilantro and *culantro* (*Eryngium foetidum*), garlic, onions, and tomatoes. Central American *sofrito*, known as *hogao*, features cumin, garlic, onions, scallions, and tomatoes (plus salt and pepper), slowly cooked to extract all their flavors—or just purchased ready-made in a bottle. Nigerian cooks have their holy trinity as well, but theirs consists of hot chiles, red onions, and tomatoes, generally cooked in palm oil. The German take on mirepoix, *suppengruen* (literally, "soup greens"), substitutes leeks for the onions and celeriac for the celery.

In the Caribbean, lard replaces the oil, and it may be colored with an-natto. The annatto imparts an orange color to the oil, mimicking the reddish palm oil that is the base of the West African equivalent of *sofrito* (an aromatic combination that usually includes onion, peppers, and tomato).

In Latin American countries, various *sofritos* take the place of mirepoix. They might include an assortment of chiles plus cilantro and *culantro*, as in Puerto Rico. Mexican *sofrito* might contain habanero chiles. The Cuban version, far less spicy, omits the chiles and replaces the herbs with bay leaves, cumin, green peppers, and oregano. When cooking beans, Cubans may add some form of cured pork (chorizo, ham, or salt pork) to their *sofrito*. That's hardly a surprise; the combination of pork and beans is almost universal—at least where pork is not a forbidden part of the diet!

Dissolving the compounds produced by cooking aromatics in a liquid is an excellent way of extracting their flavors and nutrients. What we call "flavor" is actually our brain's attempt to merge taste and scent into a single recognizable experience. Water may be the "universal solvent"—and it is the most common solvent in cooking—but alcohol and some lipids (oils) are especially effective at grabbing molecules that aren't water soluble.[7]

Szechuan hot oil. This one dissolves capsaicin and spices in soy oil. *Source:* Gary Allen

Chinese hot oil is a non-water-based example. Used as a dip or for finishing the sauce in stir-fried dishes, it is made by heating crushed red chiles (and sometimes Sichuan peppercorns) in oil. It is sometimes called "ma la oil" because the Sichuan peppercorns' hydroxy-alpha sanshool causes hot and numbing sensations ("ma" and "la," respectively). Capsaicin, the hot component of chiles, doesn't dissolve easily in water but will readily disperse in oil. The oil takes on capsaicin's heat and the pigment's (capsanthin) red coloration but remains transparent. Countless variations of this basic sauce are produced in Chinese kitchens, possibly including any number of flavoring ingredients, such as black cardamom, cinnamon, cloves, fennel, garlic, or ginger. Japan bases a similar chile-infused oil on sesame oil, and Italian *olio di peperoncino* is virtually the same thing as these hot oils (minus, of course, the Asian spices), except that olive oil replaces the sesame oil.

Vietnamese cooks make two similar oils that do not include hot chiles as dips or as sauces for noodles or rice. *Hanh la phi* is prepared by cooking scallions in oil, then straining out the solids. *Toi phi dau* is exactly the same but replaces the scallions with garlic. It's traditionally sprinkled over soups, especially those made with seafood.

In many Asian dishes, especially those from China, sesame oil is a key component. It burns easily, so it is not used for stir-frying but is added as a finishing sauce. This dark sesame oil is pressed from seeds that have first been toasted, lending a strong nutty taste that doesn't exist in the light, untoasted sesame oil one might find in a health food store. A similar fragrant finishing oil—aromatic Korean *deulgireum perilla* (*Perilla frutescens*)—is pressed from toasted seeds.

Oil appears on tables where Mediterranean foods predominate, often replacing butter as a lubricant for dry bread. It is sometimes flavored with garlic or garnished with herbs, plus black pepper or, further east, ground sumac or *za'atar* (a blend of sesame seeds and thyme-like herbs). It's the first "sauce" encountered in one's meal.

Other fats serve as sauces (or as components of other sauces). We'll be looking at vinaigrettes later, but a common Western lipid sauce is melted butter—though merely melted butter is not a proper solution. The presence of milk solids and an aqueous component disqualifies it. However, clarified butter is . . . how shall I say it . . . clear. If heated to the point at which the milk solids brown before the butter is clarified, it becomes the nutty and aromatic *beurre noisette*, or brown butter.

Filipinos cook thick coconut milk, causing its oil to separate, and continue cooking until any solids begin to brown—just as in brown butter. Since coconut milk contains more sugar than the dairy milk used to make butter, the resulting *latik* is more syrupy-sweet than *beurre noisette* and serves as a caramel-like sauce for desserts.

In Morocco, savory herbs are heated in butter before clarification, and the result is placed in pots to age (sometimes for decades) to make *smen*. The aging process creates a cheese-like pungency that is a far cry from the relatively neutral cooking fat (ghee) used in India. The Ethiopians' take on flavored ghee is *niter kibbeh*. They simmer chopped fresh garlic, ginger root, and onion in the melted butter and season it with cardamom, cinnamon, clove, fenugreek, nutmeg, and turmeric. Once the spicy clarified butter is strained into jars, it becomes a staple ingredient in classic Ethiopian dishes like *doro wat*. *Niter kibbeh* stores well, but it's not intentionally aged like *smen*.

Some of the world's oldest sauces were solutions. Mesopotamian *siqqu* and Roman *garum* are little more than fermented fish proteins dissolved in strong salty brine. To make them, merely toss a lot of small fish or scraps of

Prepared ghee and "vegetable ghee" (hydrogenated oil). *Source:* Gary Allen

larger fish into a vat with about five times their volume of salt. Weigh it down and ignore it for a few months (preferably from a comfortable location, safely upwind). Strain the resulting liquid, and there you have it. Archaeologists have unearthed *garum* "factories" all around the Mediterranean. It's much the same as the fish sauces of Asia today (such as Thai *tiparos* or Vietnamese *nước mắm*). Sauces derived from fermented seafood are almost as ubiquitous as those based on soy.

Iran has a southern coastline, and access to the sea means access to both fish and salt, so it's only natural that Iranians produce a condiment like *mahyawa*. Steeping salted anchovies along with typical local spices (the seeds of coriander, cumin, fennel, and mustard) creates the clear brown, salty, umami-rich liquid. It adds a spritz of tanginess to typical Persian flatbreads like *regag* (a thin flatbread prepared with batter, like a crepe, but cooked until light brown and crisp).

Bagoong dilis (also known as *bagoong bolinaw*, *bagoong gurayan*, and *bagoong monaman*) is a Filipino fermented anchovy paste. Anchovies, of course, are not the only small seafood that can be harvested in massive quantities, salted, fermented, and turned into protein-rich sauces. In the Philippines, the term *patís* refers to an entire class of similar sauces that are the by-product of *bagoong* making. They can be subdivided into two main categories: *bagoong isdâ* and *bagoong alamáng* (the former made from finfish, the latter from crustaceans such as krill or shrimp). There are literally dozens of *bagoong* varieties, depending on the region where they're produced, the type of seafood that is fermented, and the ratio of salt to seafood employed. *Bagoong* makers are not limited to finfish and crustaceans; mollusks (clams and oysters) also find their way into brine-filled ceramic jars. *Patís* is similar to salty umami sauces from China (*hom ha* and *yeesu*), Indonesia (*ketjap-ikan*), Japan (*ikanago-shoyu*, *ishiru*, *shottsuru*), Laos (*nam pha*), and Vietnam (*nước mắm*). *Nước mắm*, when combined with lime juice and hot chile peppers, becomes the ubiquitous *nước chấm* dipping sauce. Another name, *nước mắm pha*, refers to *nước chấm* mixed with vinegar and sweetened with sugar (palm sugar or coconut water replaces sugar in the southern parts of the country). The Thai version of *nước chấm* is called *phrik nam pla*.

Budu is a southern Thai and Malaysian fish sauce made from anchovies, while Thai *pla ra* is usually made from freshwater striped snakehead fish

(*Channa striata*). *Pla ra* is more sour than *budu* because it goes through a second fermentation in combination with rice bran and/or ground rice. Its characteristic tang is created by a specific lactobacillus (*Pediococcus halophilus*; the species name actually means "salt-loving") that feeds on the rice starches. Thais often add lime juice or tamarind to accent *pla ra*'s sourness. *Budu* gets some of its dark color from *gula kabung* (palm sugar) and tamarind. *Pla ra* is rather like the ancient Romans' *oxygarum*, a mixture of fish sauce and vinegar. The Romans sweetened *garum* by mixing the fish sauce with wine (to make *oenogarum*) or, to make it even sweeter, with honey (*meligarum*). The Korean equivalents are *mulchi aecjeot* (the liquid from fermented anchovies) and *kkanari aecjeot* (made from sand lance, *Ammodytes* spp.).

Colaturi di alici,[8] an anchovy sauce from Campania, may have come down to us directly from Roman *garum* and *liquamen*, but another descendant is much more familiar: Worcestershire sauce.

In the 1830s, Lea & Perrins first attempted to create a seasoning liquid something like what colonials had experienced in the Indian subcontinent. They failed, but their vile experiment was left in a barrel in the basement and forgotten for a couple of years—until a surprised taster discovered what has since become one of the world's best-known condiments. It is based on fermented anchovies, of course, but contains dozens of other ingredients, among them vinegars and tamarind extract, so its salty flavor-enhancing tang serves Westerners just as *pla ra* does Thais. Anchovy essence—anchovies steeped in oil and a few spices—is a simpler umami bomb.

The different styles of Japanese fish sauces are regional variations on generic salty fermented sauces, collectively known as *hishia* (or *gyosho*; *gyo* just means "fish"). Most are made from *hatahata*, a type of sand fish (*Arctoscopus japonicus*), but *ishiru* is made from sardines. The best pale, salty *shottsuru* is aged for ten years. These sauces are sometimes called *uoshoyu* (fish soy sauce) and *ikanago-shoyu* (soy sauce from sand eels, *Ammodytes personatus Girard*), revealing the fact that they add salt and umami to dishes in the same way that soy-based sauces do.

Soy sauce is made in similar fashion, but soybeans and/or wheat provide the protein. These fermented sauces don't begin as solutions, but after long aging, the solids settle out, leaving transparent (but darkly colored) solutions. The fermentation process produces hundreds of flavor components, including a little alcohol. Worcestershire sauce is prepared in a similar fashion but contains several other flavoring ingredients—again, long aging deposits any suspended particles at the bottom of the barrels (or, today, giant tanks). Some soy sauces—Korean soy sauce, *ganjang*, for example—are merely the by-products of producing fermented seasoning pastes.

Cheap soy sauce is not made by traditional fermentation; soy protein is hydrolyzed with acids, after which sugars (often corn syrup), salt, flavorings, and artificial color (usually made from soluble caramel) are added. That kind of soy sauce lacks the distinctive flavors and aromas of the hundreds of varieties of traditional sauces.

The two primary Chinese versions are thin (or light) soy, which is the saltier of the two—not to be confused with western "lite" soy sauce, which has reduced sodium content—and dark (or black) soy, which is sweetened and colored with molasses. Japanese soy (*shoyu*) tends to use more wheat in its brewing; it's milder, lighter in color, and has a little more alcohol. The most common of the lighter types is *usukuchi*; the darker is *koikuchi*. Other Japanese soy sauces include tamari (which is fermented from very little wheat, relative to its soybean content) and *shiro* (Japanese for "white"), whose ingredient ratio is the reverse of tamari's.

Korean soy sauce, *ganjang*, is similar in flavor to Japanese-style sauces. Indonesian soy sauces are called *kecap* (which has given us our word "ketchup")—though the term refers to any Indonesian fermented sauce. Like Chinese dark soy, *kecap manis* is a thick, dark liquid, but it is sweetened with jaggery (palm sugar). Thai sweet soy is similar; it's very thick and tastes like a very savory version of molasses. These thick sauces are used both as an ingredient in cooking and as a condiment (dipping sauce) at the table. *Kecap asin*, made from black beans, is saltier than other Indonesian soys.

Perhaps the most unusual take on "soy sauce" is Singapore's *angmo daoiu*, which is Southern Min for "white"—literally "redhaired man's soy sauce" (*angmo* is a racial epithet denigrating Caucasians). Angmo daoiu is, in fact a name for Worcestershire sauce! A more ethnically neutral term—*la jiangyou* ("spicy soy sauce")—is preferred in Shanghai.[9]

Soy sauce is the basis of countless sauces throughout the cuisines of East and Southeast Asia and the Pacific. It's often combined with other solutions—such as mirin (sweet rice wine) and dissolved sugar or honey for Japanese *teriyaki*. *Tentsuyu*, a dipping sauce that accompanies tempura in

Japan, combines three solutions: soy sauce, rice wine (either mirin or sake), and dashi (stock made from kombu seaweed and dried bonito flakes).

Recipe: Red Cooking

Ingredients

1 qt.	water
½ cup	Shaoxing rice wine
3 Tbsp.	dark soy
3 Tbsp.	sugar

Method

1. Combine all ingredients and bring to a boil.
2. Add browned meat, lower heat, cover, and simmer until tender and deeply colored.

   Note: The flavor of this braising liquid can be modified by adding ginger, star anise, or five spice powder.[10]

   The cook will always save the remaining gravy [sauce], add water and seasoning to it, and use it to cook other foods, removing some of that sauce in turn to be used elsewhere. The oftener it is used, the richer and more fully flavored the sauce becomes. A sauce of this sort can be kept going almost indefinitely, sometimes even for generations. The Chinese call such a preparation a master sauce.[11]

When bacteria consume an alcohol, vinegar is produced (winemakers go to elaborate lengths to prevent fruit flies from contaminating the fermenting juice with *Acetobacter aceti*). The alcohol can come from any source, each of which produces a vinegar with a different flavor and degree of acidity.

Virtually any type of fruit can be fermented (to produce red and white wines, champagne, sherry, sake, and hard cider), and the alcohol can be bacterially fermented to produce vinegar. The fruit's character affects the resulting vinegar's flavor and acidity. Examples include apples and pears (for cider vinegars); cherries (in Modena, Italy, cherry vinegar is aged in barrels made of cherry wood, yielding a dark balsamic-like vinegar); jujubes (a type of date, *Ziziphus jujuba*, for Chinese *zaocu*); persimmons (for South Korean *gam sikcho*); pineapples (for *vinaigre de piña*, ameliorated with brown sugar and used primarily in Central America); and quinces. For familiar raspberry vinegar (and similar vinegars made with black currants, blackberries, blueberries, loganberries, and strawberries), the fruit is macerated in some other vinegar, and then filtered out. Most of these vinegars are used as sauces, as they are, or as components of vinaigrettes (but then, of course, they are no longer solutions; they're emulsions).

Coconut water or sap can be fermented (after adding sugar from another source) and the resulting brew inoculated with a mass of bacteria, called a "mother," to produce vinegar. However, the much sweeter sap of date palms is a more productive method in the tropics (wine made from date palm sap is popular all over Africa and in the Philippines). Not surprisingly, dates have been used for that purpose in the Middle East from the beginning of recorded history. Since most of that region is Islamic today, date vinegar is much more prevalent there than date alcohol.

Classic balsamic vinegar, from Modena, is slowly aged in a series of barrels made of different aromatic woods, so that it gradually takes on all their flavors and thickens due to evaporation. This vinegar can be used as a sauce in its own right (for example, when balsamic vinegar is reduced to a thick syrup) or combined in various ways to yield new sauces.

Chinese cooks have several different vinegars in their culinary arsenal. Unlike most European vinegars, they're fermented from grain alcohols—most often rice—not fruit wines. Proceeding from light to dark, they are white rice vinegar, red rice vinegar, *tianjin duliu* vinegar, and black rice vinegar. The white version is the sourest (it has the highest acetic acid content) but still milder than Western white vinegars, most of which are produced synthetically through the distillation of wood by-products. It is generally a cooking ingredient, such as in sweet-and-sour dishes (where its acidity and absence of color are desired). White vinegar is also available in a wide range of ready-made flavored versions, with added cloves, ginger, orange peel, or sugar. Red rice vinegar (Shanxi aged vinegar) is brewed from red yeast fungus (*Monascus purpureus*) and a mixture of grains. It is a little smoky and salty and may be sweetened—and thickened—with sorghum syrup, though it is not as sweet as black vinegar. It can be brewed from any number of grains, such as barley, rice bran, or sorghum, with added salt and spices. It's frequently used as a dipping sauce for dim sum, combining three of the basic tastes of salty, sweet, and sour. Shanxi vinegar, also known as "extra aged vinegar," is a valuable product. Consequently, as with the rich balsamic vinegar of Modena, it is frequently imitated using entirely synthetic ingredients (and heavily doctored with the preservative sodium benzoate). As a general warning, if it's not expensive and not specifically labeled "preservative-free," it's probably a knockoff. *Tianjin duliu* "mature" vinegar is made from wheat and rice, plus peas and sorghum, from a recipe that dates to the fourteenth century. Like Shanxi, *tianjin duliu* has been widely imitated by bogus vinegars (at least fifty factories in the Tianjin neighborhood have been investigated by Chinese authorities). It's mild, not too acidic, and a little sweet—making it suitable for use as a dipping sauce. Black vinegar or brown rice vinegar (Chinkiang or Zhenjiang vinegar) can be made from sweet glutinous rice, millet, or even sorghum—but not, as one of its names might suggest, brown rice. Sometimes the rice is toasted, giving the vinegar a slightly smoky taste. Black vinegar is often compared with balsamic vinegar because of its richness. It's the thickest, sweetest, and least acidic; yet it has the most complex flavor of the Chinese vinegars (though it's not as sweet as the best balsamics). It's a complete sauce in itself, though it may be mixed with hot chile oil and chopped ginger, scallions, or garlic. Black vinegar is also used in cooking because Chinese sauces try to balance all the basic tastes, allowing a single dish—plus rice or noodles, of course—to provide a complete meal.

Japanese vinegars are even milder (that is, less acetic) than Chinese vinegars, though they're also made primarily from rice. There are three basic forms: plain rice vinegar (*komezu*), seasoned rice vinegar (*awasezu*), and black vinegar (*kurozu*). Unlike the Chinese versions, they are cooking ingredients, not sauces in their own right. Some Japanese vinegar is marketed as "seasoned"; it contains sake, salt, and sugar. Still other rice vinegars are made in Korea and Vietnam. Korean vinegar (*ssal-sikcho*) and Vietnamese vinegars (*giấm gạo*) are likewise used in cooking only.

However, in the Philippines—where there is a pronounced interest in sour flavors—vinegar (*suka*) is the basis of many dipping sauces, collectively known as *sawsawan*. Sugar is the source of alcohol used to make Filipinos' cane vinegar. Macerating a virtual salad of raw chile peppers, garlic, and red onions, together with some fried garlic, in cane vinegar yields *sukang maanghang*, a dipping sauce and all-purpose condiment. A light brown vinegar (*sukang iloko*), combined with dissolved salt and sugar and garnished with chopped red onion and garlic, might be served beside grilled pork belly. Filipinos employ sour flavors besides that of

Authentic Shanxi vinegar (note the absence of additives, pigment, or preservatives).
Source: Gary Allen

vinegar as well. The juice of citrus fruits—lemon-like calamondins (also known as *kalamansi*, a lime-like hybrid of mandarin orange and kumquat, *Fortunella japonica*) and key limes (*dayaps*)—and tamarinds lends acidity, either alone or in combination with vinegar.

Sweeteners have often been employed to temper the sour taste of vinegar. Italian *agrodolce* is a general term for such sweet-and-sour sauces (in French, it's *aigre-doux*). The Romans made several variations that incorporated honey and vinegar: *laser* sauces, with different assortments of herbs and spices, plus *liquamen*; *oxyporium*, similar, but sometimes without *liquamen*; and *hypotrimma*, like *laser* sauces but with added dried fruits, oil, and wine. Modern sweet-and-sour sauces include those made with *gastriques* (caramelized sugar diluted with vinegar and sometimes fruit juices). A classic example is the sauce for *canard à l'orange* (though some recipes call for thickening with starch—like Chinese restaurant sweet-and-sour sauce—which would make the sauce a gel rather than a solution). German *rotkohl* (red cabbage) is usually cooked in a sugar-vinegar solution, which provides flavor and preserves the cabbage's red color.[12]

Japanese *umeboshi*—very sour apricots (erroneously called "plums")—are generally preserved in salt. The salt draws liquid from the fruit, and the aromatic brine that accumulates becomes a condiment of its own. It contains citric acid, but even without acetic acid, it's so sour that it is colloquially known as *umezu* ("ume vinegar"). *Ponzu* sauce actually does contain some rice vinegar (along with mirin and a dose of umami from flakes of dried tuna and kombu, leathery sheets of dried kelp). Vinegar doesn't provide all of *ponzu*'s acidic punch, however; the juices of several citrus fruits add their unique tanginess: *Nanshô-daidai*, an orange-colored hybrid sour orange (*Citrus × aurantium*); green *kabasu* (*Citrus sphaerocarpa Tanaka*); tangerine-like *sudadachi ichandrin* (*Citrus sudadchi*); and yet another hybrid, *yuzu* (*Citrus ichangensis × Citrus reticulata*). *Ponzu* is often combined with soy sauce; that *ponzu shoyu* serves as a dipping condiment and as a basting liquid in the grilling of meat or fish.

Indian cuisines use a number of sour fruits in their sauces, though *vindaloos* are more likely to contain vinegar. That's because these sauces originated in Goa, which had been colonized by the Portuguese for nearly half a millennium, so wine and wine vinegar were known in Goan kitchens. A few indigenous vinegars existed in India before the colonial period, but they were mostly derived from fermented cane sugar, not wine. Catholic Goans tended to prefer vinegar, while Hindus in Goa and elsewhere acidulated their sauces with the sour juice of *kokam* berries (*Garcinia indica*). Indians similarly incorporated the sour juice of *nimbu* (a generic term for both limes and lemons) and *imli* (tamarind pulp).

Fried foods call for something astringent to render their fattiness less cloying, and vinegar serves the purpose well. British fish-and-chips is classically served with a splash of malt vinegar. "Malt vinegar" is a modern name for what was once known as *alegar*, a sour acetic liquid made from not wine but beer. Chinese dumplings, especially the fried ones, are often served with a dipping sauce made of soy sauce, ginger, and black vinegar (Chinkiang vinegar or Zhenjiang aromatic vinegar).

Filipinos also love fried foods and have a variety of dipping sauces, many containing vinegar (again, thanks to European colonial influence), but also tamarind and the juices of a number of sour citrus fruits: calamondins, lemons, and limes. The people of the Philippines are truly cosmopolitan in their gastronomy: we've already mentioned the Iberian connection, but the Chinese influence is represented by soy sauce, while Southeast Asians brought in fish sauce. One can find traces of virtually all these cuisines in a single dipping sauce.

One of the simplest by-product sauces is the vinegar in which hot peppers are packed. In Texas and some other southern states, a bottle of pickled hot peppers is kept on the table, and a few drops (or more) of the vinegar in which they sit gets sprinkled on cooked greens, such as collards, mustard greens, or turnip tops. When the level in the bottle gets low, more vinegar is added, and the bottle just keeps making more "pepper sauce."

Sometimes the cooking process creates its own solution-based sauce. When flan is cooked, the liquid that seeps out of the custard combines with caramelized sugar to create the dessert's own sauce. Au jus, a more savory example, is simply the intercellular fluid that comes out of meat as it roasts, picking up salts and tasty soluble compounds produced by Maillard reactions on the meat's surface along the way.[13] The browned deposit at the bottom of that pan is known as *suc*. It is usually enhanced by deglazing the pan with stock, wine, or vinegar and sometimes adding aromatics, like mirepoix—straining them out before serving. Most au jus sauces are not thickened with flour (otherwise they'd be gravy). If thickened with a starch that yields a clear sauce, such as arrowroot or corn starch, the sauce is known as *jus lié*.

Au jus is commonly served with the roasts that create them—prime rib being a classic example—but the sauce has more plebeian uses as well. A French dip, for example, is just a roast beef sandwich with a side of au jus for . . . ummm . . . dipping. The sandwich has nothing to do with France, other than its being served on a baguette. Likewise, Chicagoans' Italian beef has only tangential ties to Italy (it was supposedly invented in the stockyards by Italian immigrant laborers). It's a roast beef sandwich on Italian bread, sometimes garnished with Italian mixed pickles (*giardiniera*) or sautéed sweet peppers, then dipped—once, twice, or many times—in the broth in which the beef was cooked. The resulting sandwiches are described as "dipped," "juicy," or "soaked," respectively. There is even a simple version, called "gravy bread," that omits the beef (but it's not for vegetarians, who might be viewed suspiciously in the carnivorous Windy City). It's just a jus-sodden mass of bread with the same garnishes as an Italian beef. As one person said, after tasting gravy bread for the first time, "I appreciate a food that appeals to multiple generations: pre-tooth babies and post-tooth seniors. . . . I like a food that melts in my mouth, but I really prefer if it waits until it's actually in my mouth."[14]

Because of solutions' ability to extract flavor (and the ease with which they can be reduced, concentrating their flavors to an essence), they often form the basis for other sauces. If those others are "mother sauces," then solutions could well be considered the "grandmother sauces."

8

SUSPENSIONS

Suspensions differ from solutions primarily in the size of the particles dispersed in the liquid. Rather than individual molecules or ions, tiny bits of matter are suspended in the liquid portion of the sauce. Fruit or vegetable purées are typical suspensions. Unlike solutions, suspensions range from slightly cloudy to translucent to opaque—due to light scattering.

Most hot sauces, like Tabasco, are suspensions (minuscule fragments of chile peppers floating in a vinegary medium). Straining doesn't remove all of the pepper bits, which is why the sauce is cloudy, not transparent. Tabasco's newer chipotle- and habanero-based sauces contain so much suspended matter that they're opaque.

Unlike solutions' molecules, suspensions' larger particles tend to separate out of the sauce. Generally heavier than the liquid, they usually sink to the bottom (or, when a coulis[1]—a strained purée of fruit, such as raspberries—is left too long on the plate, a small ring forms as the suspending liquid gradually oozes from the mound of solids). Such sauces need to be shaken to redistribute the solids in the liquid. If, however, their size is very small—as in Tabasco—the particles may stay in suspension just by Brownian motion, being bumped around by the molecular motion of their liquid. The puréed fermented peppers in Tabasco are combined with vinegar, then vigorously mixed for twenty-eight days to reduce the particles to a size small enough to stay in suspension. No thickening ingredients are required to prevent the sauce from separating.

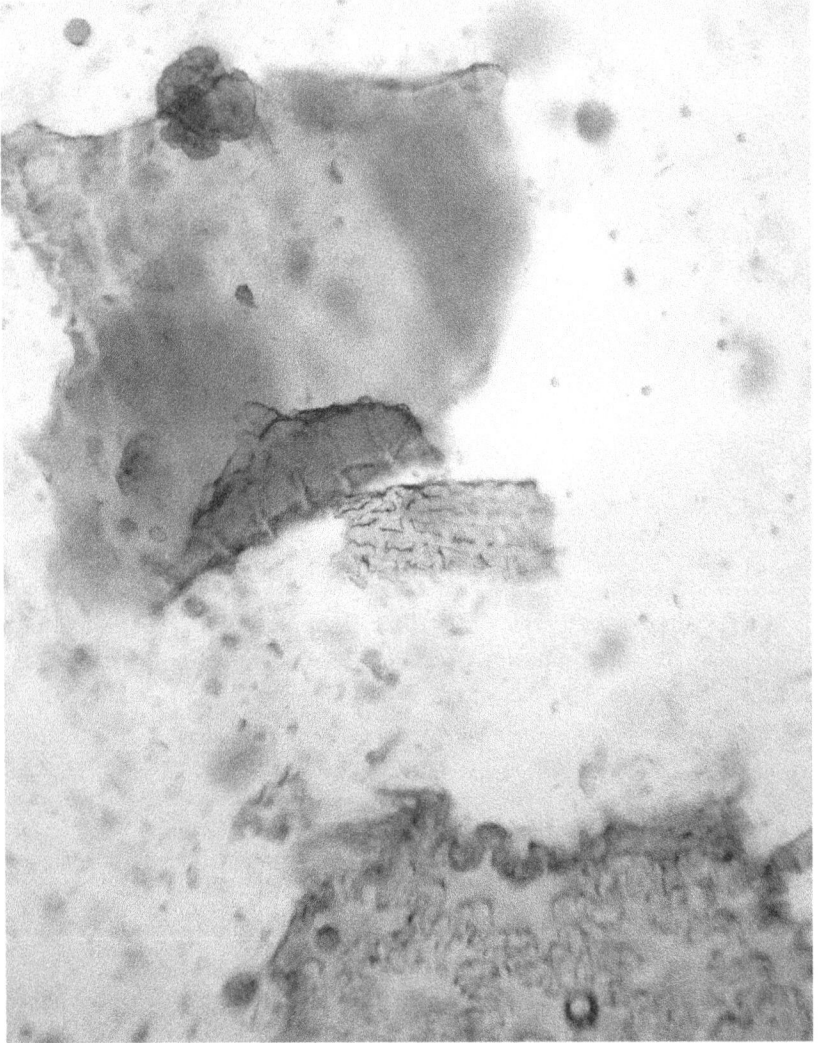

Tabasco sauce, viewed through a microscope. The dark area, top left, is a fragment of tabasco pepper. Individual cell walls can be seen in the little flap at the bottom of the fragment and in the small rectangle of skin in the center of the image. The clear white area is a solution of salt in vinegar. *Source:* Gary Allen

Many other commercial suspension-type sauces avoid separation of solid and liquid portions by adding emulsifying agents, which we'll discuss a little later.

Literally thousands of hot sauces are manufactured commercially around the world—and almost all of them qualify as suspensions. One of the most popular, in recent years, is *sriracha*. While Tabasco has been produced on Louisiana's Avery Island since the Civil War, *sriracha* has only been around since the 1930s. *Sriracha*-like sauces were originally made in Thailand for Burmese customers who had been making similar sauces at home for some time. Today it is sold under a number of brand names, but the largest supplier is Huy Fong Foods.[2] The familiar "rooster sauce" is a finely ground paste of red jalapeño peppers and garlic, suspended in a solution of salt, sugar, and white vinegar. David Tran, its creator, began making hot sauces in Los Angeles's Chinatown in 1975.[3] Before hitting on the recipe for *sriracha*, he produced chili garlic paste, *sambal badjak* (a brown condiment made of galangal, garlic, hot peppers, nutmeg, palm sugar, shrimp paste, shallots, and tamarind), *sambal oelek* (like a thicker, unsweetened version of *sriracha*), and another pepper sauce he called Sa-te.

Sa-te is his own name for Chinese *shacha*, a gritty paste of chile, garlic, shallots, soybean oil, and two kinds of seafood: brill (a flounder-like fish, *Scophthalmus rhombus*) and pungent dried shrimp. *Shacha* is a common ingredient in Chinese kitchens, not usually employed as a condiment itself. It does enliven dips to accompany Mongolian hot pots—when it's likely to be combined with Chinkiang black vinegar, more hot peppers, soy, and a mixture of chopped cilantro, garlic, and scallions.

Filipinos, whose diets often consist of fatty meats (especially pork) or fried foods (such as their egg-roll-like *lumpia*) need something to cut through all that fat. They love sour flavors, so they have created a wide range of dipping sauces, most of which are acidic solutions garnished with floating solids. The liquid varies; it could be one of the many vinegars they produce or citrus juices (like lemon, lime, or *kalamansi*). The seasoning or garnishes might include all or some of the following: black pepper, an assortment of minced hot chiles (both fresh and dried), cucumber, garlic, and onion or scallion. Filipino cooking is a prototypical fusion cuisine, so these dips might be seasoned with salt, soy sauce, or a Southeast Asian fish sauce. The following sauce is uncooked but requires aging for its flavors to develop:

Recipe: Sari Sari Sauce

Ingredients

1	whole fresh coriander plant, finely chopped
3 cloves	garlic, peeled and crushed
1–5 (to taste)	hot chiles, finely chopped
3 Tbsp.	fish sauce (such as *patís*)
3 Tbsp.	light (not "lite") soy sauce
1 Tbsp.	white wine vinegar or *kalamansi**
3	black pepper corns, cracked

* If *kalamansi* juice, fresh or bottled, is unavailable, substitute lime juice.

Method

1. Combine all ingredients in a jar. Cover.
2. Allow to macerate for at least a week before using.

Pili-pili sauce, from central Africa, contains ground chiles, garlic, and onion in sweetened and salted vinegar, thickened with tomato paste—thus it has four ingredients suspended in a three-part solution.

Salsas are hot sauces that are often prepared in the home (as opposed to prepared, bottled sauces, though many *salsas* are now sold, ready-made, in jars as well). The familiar taco sauce is a thin and finely puréed commercial product—clearly a sauce, for our purposes, but not really a *salsa*. The most common *salsa*, served in restaurants or at home to accompany chips, is *salsa roja*. It's a cooked mixture of tomatoes, chiles, onions, and garlic and is the most common topping (along with an omnipresent and inauthentic thick layer of melted cheese) for enchiladas in the United States. *Criollo* sauce, or *hogao*, a type of *salsa roja*, is made in Colombia and usually flavored with cumin. It's available as a jarred sauce in US markets—at least those that cater to Latin American customers.

Mexican *salsa verde* is usually a cooked sauce (though occasionally it may be served raw) made primarily of puréed tomatillos and chiles and some onion, whose flavors are brightened by lime juice and a bit of cilantro.

Pico de gallo is the standard Mexican restaurant fresh salsa (*salsa cruda*, or raw sauce). It's a chunky mixture of tomatoes and onions, seasoned with cilantro, cumin, garlic, jalapeño or serrano chiles, lime juice, salt, and pepper. *Chiltomate* is close but adds onion, drops the lime juice, and is hotter because it substitutes habaneros for the jalapeños or serranos. Traditionally, *salsas* are pounded in a mortar and pestle—a *molcajete*—but *pico de gallo* (or *salsa bandera*, since it has the colors of the Mexican flag) is coarsely chopped. Today, Mexican *salsas* are commonly made in a food processor or a blender—even though grinding is said to better extract the ingredients' flavors. The *jeow mak len* of Laos, a very similar dipping sauce, is more piquant due to several fresh Thai chiles and has additional salt and umami from fish sauce. Ghana's take on salsa, *kpakpo shito*, is a mixture of chile peppers, tomatoes, onion, and salt, pounded in a mortar.

Mexico has its own dipped sandwich, but unlike the French dip sandwich described in the last chapter, it is served with salsa rather than au jus. *Tortas ahogadas*, literally "drowned sandwiches," are soggy masses from Guadalajara. As in so many other culinary "histories," they were supposedly invented by accident—when a cook dropped a sandwich into a vat of salsa. The story is reminiscent of the one in which the first chimichanga came into being when a burrito fell into a fryer filled with hot fat. Sometimes these stories are true, but more often they should be taken with a side of salsa.

In the Canary Islands an entire class of *salsas*—called *mojos*—employs reconstituted dried red chiles or fresh green ones. The ingredients are finely chopped and combined with different spices (coriander, cumin, garlic, paprika), oil, and something sour, such as citrus juices or vinegar. Variations include one with pounded almonds (reflecting the Spanish roots of Canarian cuisine) or locally grown saffron. Émigrés from the Canaries brought their taste for *mojos* to the Caribbean. Cubans, Dominicans, and Puerto Ricans each have their own versions of *mojo*, though in the Dominican Republic *mojo* is known as *wasakaka*.

The Middle East has another take on *salsas*: *zhug* (or *sahawiq* or *skhug*). Examples can include tomatoes, but most are based on hot peppers, along with cardamom, cloves, coriander, cumin, garlic, and sometimes caraway seeds. It's a looser and coarser version of *harissa* (a North African paste of hot chiles and various spices, such as the seeds of coriander and caraway), ground in oil. The Israeli version, *filfel chuma*, sometimes includes lemon juice. Most ready-made *harissa* is sold in various types of containers (commonly small tubes), and Tunisia is the main exporter. The *muhammara* prepared by Iraqis, Syrians, and Turks is thickened with breadcrumbs and/or ground walnuts—and is a little tarter, as it adds lemon juice or pomegranate molasses. *Ajika*, made in Georgia, skips the acidic juices of *muhammara* but adds blue fenugreek (*Trigonella caerulea*). The simpler Turkish sauce, *biber salçası*, is both condiment and ingredient. It's a loose paste of sun-dried peppers and salt and comes in two forms: *acı* and *tatlı*, hot or sweet, respectively. *Ajvar* (*ajbap*, Serbian vegetable caviar) is a Balkan version. It's mostly sweet red peppers with some eggplant, garlic, and a bit of hot chile.

Other Middle Eastern dishes that border on dips include hummus and *baba ganoush* (described in chapter 4). They are scooped up with each region's traditional flatbread. The latter is slightly thinner than hummus. The eggplant develops a smoky taste after being roasted to the point of collapse. A Persian variation on *baba ganoush*, called *naz khatoon*, adds a salted pesto-like mixture of herbs, *dalal* (typically basil, cilantro, and parsley); replaces the lemon juice with verjuice to brighten the taste; and is garnished with chopped walnuts to provide a little crunch.

Lebanese *tarator* is similarly tahini based and also includes garlic and lemon juice, but it's simpler, lacking either chickpeas or eggplant. It is garnished with chopped parsley. *Ab-doogh-khiar*, an Iranian take on *tarator*, suspends bits of basil, ground black pepper, and minced leeks, garnished with chopped mint and raisins.

French *mignonette* serves a purpose much like that of *salsas* but traditionally accompanies raw oysters. The name also refers to cracked black pepper—which is a key ingredient. Minced shallots and vinegar make up the balance of the recipe for this sauce.

Today most suspensions have their suspended matter broken into tiny fragments using machines, such as food processors. Before that, hand-operated food mills forced vegetable pulp through screens, basically the same process as that employed by Guillaume Tirel with his *tamis*. If we go further back, the method was truly ancient: pounding with a mortar and pestle. Many still consider this to be the best method, as pounding extracts more flavorful juice than processes that rely on cutting the food, no matter how finely.

There can be no better exemplar than *pesto alla genovese*. Its very name is a commandment to break out the mortar and pestle. Classically, the sauce is just fresh basil, garlic, salt, olive oil, and pine nuts, pounded together then combined with cheeses: Parmigiano-Reggiano and *pecorino sardo*. Of course, many other pestos can be prepared in the same manner; other herbs, arugula, mint, or parsley may be combined with almonds or walnuts.

Oysters on the half shell, with a little cup of mignonette dipping sauce. *Source:* Gary Allen

Other Italian variations on *pesto alla genovese* include *pesto alla calabrese* and *pesto alla siciliana*. The first replaces most of the basil with sweet red peppers that are first grilled, then pounded together with garlic, onion, and tomato, and *pecorino sardo* gives way to mild and creamy ricotta. The second goes further, adding salty *ricotta salata*, pine nuts, and almonds, as well as crushed red pepper for a bit of heat. It has much more basil than *pesto alla calabrese*.

Pistou, which is pesto minus the cheese, is used as an ingredient in, or condiment for, Provençal dishes. Another Provençal form of pesto, made from anchovies, capers, and black olives, is known as *tapenade*. It is some-times brightened with lemon juice or spiked with brandy. *Persillade* replaces the basil in *pistou* with parsley and acidulates it with vinegar.

Pesto and *pistou* are by no means the only green sauces. "Green sauces" exist in many places, and while they are all served cold and all are, in essence, minced herbs in suspension, they are very different from each other. To start, an Italian green sauce that isn't pesto: chopped anchovies, capers, garlic, onion, and parsley, suspended in olive oil and thickened with vinegar-soaked bread. The French version adds tarragon and replaces vinegar with lemon juice. Here's a sixteenth-century recipe by Bartolomeo Scappi:

Historic Recipe: To Prepare Green Sauce

Get parsley, spinach tips, sorrel, burnet, rocket and a little mint; chop them up small and grind them in a mortar with thin slices of toast. It is optional whether you put in almonds or hazelnuts, though for the sauce to be greener you should not. When that is ground up, put in pepper and salt, moistening it with vinegar. If it is thoroughly ground up, there is no need to strain it. It can be made in the same way with vine sprouts—that is grape-vine tendrils.[4]

While green goddess dressing is thickened by mayonnaise (an emulsion of raw egg and oil), German *grüne soße* (literally, "green sauce") gets its viscosity from mashed hard-boiled eggs and its color from a combination of fresh herbs—the exact mixture of which varies from town to town—such as borage, chervil, chives, dill, garden cress, lemon balm, lovage, parsley, sorrel, *salad burnet*, and sometimes spinach or wild greens, plus shallots, in the usual oil and vinegar. The Germans really depart from French and Italian cooks by stirring in sour cream (or buttermilk, or *quark*, or yogurt), then thickening the mixture with sieved hard-boiled eggs.

Sauce gribiche is a somewhat green sauce that looks like an emulsion but really isn't. To make it, sieve hard-boiled egg yolks, mix with mustard, and beat the mixture into a mild-flavored oil. At this point it resembles mayonnaise, but when you add chopped pickles and capers, along with minced herbs (chervil, parsley, and tarragon), all resemblance to the other green sauces vanishes. It is classically served with delicately flavored proteins, like poached fish or chicken, and garnished with the whites of the hard-boiled eggs, coarsely chopped.

Sauce verte au pain, a simple suspension that dates back to the Renaissance, also featured hard-boiled eggs and some bread as thickeners. Its liquid ingredients were white wine vinegar (perhaps verjuice, originally) and oil. The suspended flavorings were minced capers, chives, cornichons, and parsley.

The *chimichurris* of Argentina and Uruguay are predominantly herbal *salsas*; they replace tomatoes with lots of parsley, sharpened with vinegar and oil. *Pebre* is the Chilean version, while *llajwa* is Bolivian; both are ground on flat stone *batans* (similar to the *metates* used to grind masa in Mexico). Throughout the Caribbean, a salsa is known as a *mojo*. These sauces are thinner, serving as both dips and marinades. Their characteristic tropical flavor results from combining the juices of oranges and limes instead of vinegar.

Simple mint sauces, with fresh herbs pounded in vinegar (and sometimes sweetened for use in desserts), accompany lamb in Great Britain and Ireland—as mint jelly does in the United States. Such sauces were common in the Middle Ages but have been largely replaced by other forms of pesto today.

In the North African cooking of Algeria, Libya, Morocco, and Tunisia, *chermoula* is the herb-in-oil sauce of preference. Beginning with a suspension of finely chopped cilantro in olive oil and lemon juice, regional variations take off in all directions. Spices might include black pepper, chiles, cloves, coriander seeds, cumin, and/or saffron. Aromatic ingredients like garlic, onions, parsley, and preserved lemons might be added.

While hot sauces are popular condiments based on suspensions, tomato ketchup is probably the most familiar. Ironically, the original ketchup didn't have tomatoes, nor was it a suspension. *Kê-chiap* was a Chinese sauce, a salty solution of fermented fish, much like Roman *liquamen* or Vietnamese *nam pla*. Chinese influence led to its being adopted in Indonesia, where English traders discovered it. Laotian *padaek*, a slightly thicker fermented sauce made from freshwater fish, follows the familiar pattern, but it often contains bits of suspended fish flesh.

Not really understanding how the sauce was produced or having access to the same ingredients that produced the umami-rich liquid, English households adapted it as best they could to local circumstances. They substituted mushrooms for the fish, accidentally matching the high level of glutamate found in the original sauce (some early British and American recipes strained out all solids, leaving a dark savory liquid, something like Worcestershire, that is closer to a solution than a suspension). It may be hard to believe today, but mushroom catsup was once incredibly popular. Crosse & Blackwell sold seventeen thousand gallons of the stuff in 1857.[5] They also made ketchup from pickled unripe walnuts.

Historic Recipe: Walnut Ketchup

Ingredients—100 green walnuts, 1 quart of good vinegar, 3 ozs. of salt, 4 ozs. of anchovies, 12 finely-chopped shallots, ½ stick of finely-grated horseradish, ½ teaspoonful each of mace, nutmeg, ground ginger, ground cloves, and pepper, 1 pint of port.

Method—The walnuts must be very young and tender. Bruise them slightly, put them into a jar with the salt and vinegar, and let them remain for 8 days, stirring them daily. Drain the liquor from them into a stewpan, add to it the rest of the ingredients, simmer very gently for 40 minutes, and when cold strain the preparation into small bottles. Cork them closely, cover with melted wax, and store in a cool, dry place.[6]

Both versions found their way to the American colonies. Food historian Karen Hess wrote, "Until after the mid-nineteenth century, ketchup in American cookbooks was assumed to be of either mushrooms or oysters unless otherwise specified. The earliest published recipe for *tomato catsup* that I know is given by Mary Randolph in *The Virginia Housewife*, 1824, who also gives one for tomato soy (a name that became popular), that differs little from the other."[7] Note the spelling "catsup," which is still in use in parts of the southern United States. Also note that oysters were used—a throwback to the sauce's origins. Finally, the use of "soy" is another nod to Asian condiments loaded with umami (which Europeans had long found confusing; remember that Jean Antheleme Brillat-Savarin thought soy sauce came from India!).

Historic Recipe: Oyster Catsup

Get fine fresh oysters, wash them in their own liquor, put them in a marble mortar with salt, pounded mace, and cayenne pepper, in the proportions of one ounce salt, two drachms [1 drachm = ⅛ ounce] mace, and one of cayenne to each pint of oysters; pound them together, and add a pint of white wine to each pint; boil it some minutes, and rub it through a sieve; boil it again, skim it, and when cold, bottle, cork, and seal it. This composition gives a fine flavour to white sauces, and if a glass of brandy be added, it will keep good for a considerable time.[8]

Eliza Smith's *The Compleat Housewife* (1742) included five recipes with "catchup" (and one with "ketchup") as an ingredient. Her version of the

Nineteenth-century label for a ketchup bottle. *Source:* Public domain

sauce was a mixture of anchovies, cloves, ginger, and mace, all boiled in white wine. The only reason it might be considered a suspension was the presence of grated horseradish (as horseradish root is insoluble, it is invariably a component of suspension-type sauces, such as mustard and Japanese wasabi). It had to be aged in the bottle for at least a week. The fermentation recapitulates the sauce's historical connection to ancient fish sauces.

Historic Recipes: Camp Ketchups

1. Anchovies, 4 oz., mix with beer, 2 quarts, white wine, 1 quart, boil a short time, add peeled shalots, 3 oz., black pepper, mace, nutmegs, and ginger, of each, ½ oz.; macerate for 14 days, and bottle.
2. Vinegar, 2 pints, walnut ketchup, 1 pint, mushroom ketchup, 3 oz., garlic, 4 cloves, Cayenne pods, ½ oz., soy, 2 oz., wine, 4 oz., 3 anchovies, 1 oz. salt. Macerate together 3 weeks, and bottle.
3. Vinegar, 1 pint, walnut-ketchup, 4 oz., soy, 2 oz., 12 chopped anchovies, 2 cloves of garlic, and Cayenne pods, 1 drachm; macerate three weeks, and bottle.[9]

Once ketchup began being made of tomatoes, it never looked back (British mushroom and walnut ketchups are still available, but they are only a marginal part of the ketchup phenomenon). Early tomato ketchup recipes still contained anchovies, and they were still fermented, but by the early nineteenth century both practices had been abandoned. Instead, makers added vinegar (to make up for the lost tang of fermentation) and sugar (to soften the effect of vinegar, to better preserve the bottled sauce . . . and because everyone loves sugar!). The addition of sugar has, more than any other factor, made ketchup the universal condiment that it has become (although tomatoes are also a potent source of glutamates).

Before the nineteenth century, ketchup was produced only in home kitchens. With the advent of commercial canning, ketchup production moved almost entirely to factories. In recent years, "artisanal" or "housemade" ketchups have appeared sporadically, but they have never replaced the familiar tapered bottles found on tables everywhere. These ersatz, and somewhat pretentious, ketchups are even the butt of snarky attack articles.

> No matter how hard you try, you can't beat what Henry John Heinz bottled back in 1876. You can't fancy it up. Or actually, you CAN, but that's the first step on a short road directly to insignificance. Heinz's flavor collisions are, very literally and possibly scientifically, perfect. Our mouths love umami—that evasive but very real fifth basic taste—and Heinz has a shitload of it.[10]

That ketchup is, in fact, a suspension is documented in US Department of Agriculture (USDA) standards. The grading system used for ketchup is based upon the percentage of solids (particles of tomato) it contains. The highest rating, "fancy," is given to ketchups that are 33 percent solids. The lowest rating, "standard," has only 25 percent solids. If your ketchup pours from the bottle too easily, it's not "fancy" (though commercial producers add xanthan gum to increase ketchup's viscosity, so one can be easily fooled).

Tomato ketchup use has spread around the world. During World War II, tomatoes were in short supply in the Philippines, so María Y. Orosa (a food technologist turned guerilla who was accidentally killed by American artillery fire in 1945) substituted bananas and mangoes. The resulting products became Filipino staples (which are sometimes dyed red to imitate their tomato forbears). In fact, tomato ketchup never really regained its place on Filipinos' tables or in their kitchens. However, bananas are not the only fruit used to make ketchup-like sauces. Plums yield a sour condiment called *themali*. It is sweet, sour, and spicy and plays the same role as ketchup in Georgia (of the Caucasus, not the southern US state).

In Mexico, a sweet and tart condiment that somewhat resembles ketchup is common on street foods. The eponymous sauce was originally made from a fruit called *chamoy* that was introduced by Asian immigrants before the nineteenth century. Like Japanese *umeboshi* and Chinese *li hing mui* or *huamei* (a kind of sour plum or apricot), various fruits—typically apricots, mangoes, or plums—are salted or soaked in brine. The fruits can be eaten, as is, like candy—or their pickling liquid can be thickened with fruit purée, spiced with chile, and acidulated with vinegar. The resulting *chamoy* sauces are sold in varying viscosities; thin ones are like bottled hot sauces, somewhat thicker ones are employed like ketchup, and the thickest ones are like the dips Americans might serve with crudités. *Chamoy*, always dyed a bright red, is so popular that ersatz versions, devoid of any fruit, flood the market—and since the color is expected to be artificial, who would be the wiser?

Ketchup (whether tomato, mushroom, or banana) is often an ingredient in cooking (just as it was in Eliza Smith's day). We'll see more on this later, but just think how common it is in sauces for barbecue or in "cocktail sauce" served with seafood, when it is combined with horseradish (and sometimes Tabasco). It has even found its way back into Chinese kitchens, where it is often a component of the sweet-and-sour dishes so common on ordinary takeout menus.

Mustard is second only to ketchup in the pantheon of common condiments. All mustards start with seeds (of various colors and *Brassica* species). The suspended particles of ground powdered mustard or whole seeds, or a combination of the two, produce a variety of textures and flavors.

The seeds must be macerated in a liquid (typically beer, vinegar, water, or wine), but not merely to extract their flavor. The maceration actually *produces* the hot flavor. The name "mustard" reflects this process, since it derives from the Latin *mustum*—the unfermented grape juice used to develop the ground seeds' heat. Mustard gets its heat from a very different set of compounds than are found in hot peppers (or even true pepper). Rather than from capsaicin (in chiles) or piperine (in black pepper), mustard's burn comes from acrinyl isothiocyanate (in white mustard, *Brassica hirta*) or allyl isothiocyanate (in black mustard, *Brassica nigra*; in brown mustard, *Brassica juncea*). None of these compounds exist in the seeds themselves; they are created when the seeds are broken in the presence of some form of moisture. That releases the enzyme myrosinase and several other compounds

Nineteenth-century label for a mustard jar. *Source:* Public domain

(glucosinolates; the types and relative amounts in different species account for their differing flavors and intensities) in the seeds that, when combined, produce their burning sensation. In addition to the compounds that deliver its heat, mustard also contains some lecithin and a form of mucilage—a gelatinous polysaccharide—that aid in thickening any sauce to which it is added.

The temperature and acidity of the liquid determine how much isothiocyanate can be produced in those reactions. If the temperature is too high or the pH is too low, the mustard won't be hot. Excess heat can destroy the myrosinase before it has a chance to react with the glucosinolates. Hence, it is crucial that the seeds not be heated too much by the friction of milling them. Before the eighteenth century, all mustard sauces were composed of whole or lightly crushed seeds. This recipe, from the fourteenth century's *The Book of Sent Soví*, would not have been as fiery as today's mustards.

Historic Recipe: Mostalla

Mustard our way: grind the mustard [seeds] and crush them, or grind them in a mill. Scald two or three times, and then grind it and mix with cold broth. And put in honey or sugar.

If you want to make some in the French way, mix it with vinegar. And you can put in fruit syrup.[11]

Clearly, honey mustard is not a new idea!

In 1720, a Mrs. Clements found a way to grind the seeds, removing their husks, without creating undue heat. Within a century, Jeremiah Colman was able to market a type of finely ground powder that is the basis for all modern mustards. The hottest purely mustard-based sauces are found in Chinese restaurants. They are nothing but a thick suspension of Colman-type[12] powdered mustard in water that is allowed to rest before serving. Much hotter are the scotch bonnet sauces, from Barbados and other West Indian islands, whose inhabitants use mustard as a thickener for their incendiary condiments.

The "wasabi" usually served with sushi in most Japanese restaurants is prepared from a mixture of powdered mustard and ground dried horseradish (and some green food coloring), mixed with water a little before serving to develop its flavor. True wasabi is rare and costly and made by grating a fresh root of *Wasabia japonica*.

Any cooked dishes that feature the heat of mustard (such as barbecue sauces, especially those from South Carolina, or simple pan sauces) must be made from mustard seeds that have already developed their isothiocyanate. This is generally accomplished by simply adding prepared mustard (though it could be done by adding mustard powder to liquid and letting it rest before cooking).

Hundreds of prepared mustards exist around the world; entire books have been written about them, so we'll only touch on their varieties.

American mustard comes in two basic forms: yellow mustard (usually just called "mustard") and spicy brown mustard. Yellow mustard—such as French's—is relatively mild and vinegary; in our house we call it "baby mustard." It contains less mustard powder (from white mustard seeds), so it is generally thickened with a starch. Spicy brown mustard—such as Gulden's—is coarser, with bits of brown mustard seeds visible. Some spicy brown mustards add the zip of horseradish. Many varieties of honey mustard can be found on American grocery shelves—but unlike the basic mustards, which are fairly straightforward preparations, they often contain many additives, such as high-fructose corn syrup, sugar, modified corn starch, xanthan gum, invert sugar, and sodium benzoate.

French—as opposed to French's—mustards are not bright yellow (they don't contain turmeric). Originally made with verjuice, the tart juice of unripe grapes, most are made with white wine. Dijon mustard (named for the Burgundian town that is the center of Gallic mustard production) is finely ground brown mustard seeds, moistened with wine. Grey Poupon, the brand best known in the United States, is named not for its less-intense coloration but for the two men who founded the company in the eighteenth century. Another French producer is Maille (making dozens of types, from simple Dijon mustard, to whole grain mustards, to special ones incorporating expensive ingredients, like chanterelles, cognac, morels, or black truffles). Pommery (another eighteenth-century company) makes Moutarde de Meaux. Unlike most French mustards, it does not come from Dijon—Meaux is in the Île-de-France region, near Paris, where a type of Brie is made. Its label boasts the mustard quote attributed to Brillat-Savarin, though producers from Dijon or Düsseldorf might disagree.

ABB (Adam Bernhard Bergrath) began making mustard in Düsseldorf about fifty years before Maurice Grey and Auguste Poupon set up their shop in Dijon. The coarse-ground mustard of Düsseldorf was made from a mixture of seed types and macerated in vinegar instead of wine. If it seems familiar to American diners, that's because the common spicy brown mustard is based on an old Düsseldorf recipe.

Horseradish also gets its distinctive bite from allyl isothiocyanate, which forms when the fresh root is ground, breaking its cellular structure and allowing the catalytic reactions seen in mustards. "Prepared horseradish" is grated root in vinegar. It's too coarse to be a true suspension, but the minimal amount of liquid makes it seem like a suspension. In the United Kingdom, lemon juice may replace the vinegar in "horseradish sauce," a term that has a different meaning in the United States. There, "prepared horseradish" is sometimes sold dyed deep red with beet juice, a style that is popular in Poland and other parts of Eastern Europe. Russian *khrenovina* is like American cocktail sauce on steroids; tomatoes and horseradish are ground together with garlic, pepper, salt, and anything else Russians believe will enhance a sauce they rightly call *gorloder*, the "throat throttler." No doubt, ice-cold vodka is the antidote of choice.

In many South Indian recipes, whole mustard seeds are toasted or fried, thereby destroying the myrosinase. They provide a pleasant nutty flavor but no heat to the sauce. *Kasundi*, however, is quite hot. It's a form of relish originally made of fermented mustard seeds. Many versions today add canned tomato products, sugar, and vinegar. Chicago chef Tim Graham once described it as "ketchup with a lot more going on."[13]

When using ketchup or mustard just doesn't seem right—such as when there's a steak on our plate—we have a number of suspension-type condiments from which to choose. These so-called steak sauces are generally as brown as Worcestershire but much thicker. Most of them originated in Great Britain and migrated to the New World.

A.1. steak sauce was first produced commercially in 1831, though it didn't acquire that name until 1868. The H. W. Brand Company showed it at an international cuisine exposition, where it earned the description "A.1."—hence the name by which it will always be remembered. A long series of corporate mergers concluded with its belonging to the American conglomerate Kraft Foods in 1999. The sauce is based on vinegar, but its suspended ingredients include a purée of oranges, raisins, sultanas, and tomatoes flavored with garlic, onion, and spices. It is sweetened with corn syrup, darkened with caramel coloring, and thickened with xanthan gum.

A similar British product (which has since become Americanized) is HP Sauce. It and a few similar competitors—known collectively as "brown sauce"—completely replaced A.1. in England, but HP is still a big seller in America, Australia, and Canada. It consists of malt vinegar and a suspension of ground dates and tomatoes, flavored by some unspecified spices and given a sour bite by tamarind extract (like Worcestershire sauce). Originally produced by Frederick Gibson Garton in 1895, the sauce is now made by Heinz in Canada, Mexico, and the Netherlands. Heinz 57 is somewhat different. It is closer to ketchup, albeit with added mustard, which gives it a brighter, more yellow-orange color than other steak sauces.

Another brown suspension, Pickapeppa, hails from Jamaica. First produced in 1921, it has a vinegar base (fermented from cane sugar), sweetened with more sugar. Its suspended components are mangoes, onions, peppers, raisins, and tomatoes. It's seasoned with black pepper, cloves, garlic, ginger, orange zest, sea salt, and thyme. While the name sounds like the sauce would have a hot flavor, it doesn't; it actually tastes a lot like A.1. For those who prefer something more piquant, Pickapeppa makes a hotter version that includes Scotch bonnet peppers.

Elsewhere in the Caribbean region, one can sample many local sauces based on Scotch bonnets. While ripe habaneros are red, Scotch bonnets are usually yellow-orange in color, so the sauces are school-bus yellow. Many of these sauces are thickened with mustard and/or a purée of carrots that accentuates the tropical color and fruitiness of the peppers.

Umami-laden sauces based on dried fish are not unique to ancient Rome and Great Britain. Chinese *shacha* sauce is commonly used as a condiment, by itself, or as a component of dips, rubs, and soups in Fujian, Guangdong, and Taiwan. The sauce consists of dried shrimp and dried local flat fish, pounded in oil with chiles, garlic, and shallots. The Taiwanese call it "barbecue sauce." They make a dipping sauce of it with chiles, Chinkiang black vinegar, cilantro, garlic, scallions, sesame oil, and soy sauce. On the other side of the globe, Ghanaians make the very similar *shito* from various dried crustaceans (crayfish, shrimp, or prawns), smoke-dried bonga shad (*Ethmalosa fimbriata*), garlic, and onions, with some added chiles and tomato paste. Curiously, it's served on tables in Chinese restaurants in Ghana as a substitute for the usual hot ma la oil.

The *sambals* of Indonesia, Malaysia, and Sri Lanka are yet more examples of this type of chili-garlic-ginger-scallion-shallot-dried-fish suspension. They are traditionally ground in a mortar and pestle, producing a coarse purée of suspended spices and protein. Hundreds of variations on the condiment's basic recipe exist in the region—some raw, some cooked, some with fresh or fermented fruits, thickened with different types of nuts (candlenuts, coconuts), and containing a variety of dried fishes, as well as, of course, one or more of the six types of chiles grown in the area.

Nam chims are Thai dipping sauces; they are very fluid and used primarily for dipping foods such as grilled meats and fried fishcakes. Thai cooks start their *nam chims* and curries with chile pastes (*nam phriks*) and curry pastes (*krung gaeng*). The latter come in five basic varieties (as close as Thai cuisine comes to a system of mother sauces): red, orange, green, yellow, and *mussaman*.

Red curry paste (*krung gaeng ped*) gets its color from fresh, ripe *prik e noo* (Thai chiles, also called "bird chiles" or "mouse-dropping chiles" because of their size; *Capsicum minimum*) and/or the dried version (*prik haeng*). It also contains salt, garlic, lemongrass, fresh turmeric root, and *kapi* (preserved shrimp paste).

Orange curry paste (*krung gaeng som*) contains *prik chi fa* (spur chile peppers; *Capsicum annuum acuminatum*), garlic, and shallots, plus sour tamarind juice and/or rice vinegar; *kapi* and fish sauce provide umami. It also includes the rhizomes of *krachai* (lesser galangal; *Kæmpferia galanga*), a resinous relative of ginger.

Green curry paste (*krung gaeng keo wan*) uses very hot fresh green chiles, called *prik e noo*, and herbs such as coriander root[14] and lemongrass; spices like the seeds of caraway, coriander, and cumin; cloves and nutmeg; aromatics such as *ka* (galangal), *makrut*[15] lime peel, garlic, *krachai*, and shallots; salt and black pepper; and a dose of umami from *kapi*.

Ready-made green curry paste. *Source:* Gary Allen

Yellow curry paste (*krung gaeng lueang*)[16] and *mussaman* curry paste (*gaeng mussaman kaa*) are very similar, though the former is strongly colored with turmeric. They feature sweet spices, like cardamom, cinnamon, cloves, coriander seed, and star anise; the heat comes from red chiles and white pepper, and aromatic properties are the result of cumin, galangal, garlic, *makrut* lime peel, lemongrass, and shallots. They also get plenty of umami from *kapi* and fish sauce. The *mussaman* name and the sweet spices—not much used in Thai cooking—show the influence of ancient trade with Indian Muslims.

These sauces are prepared, at home, by pounding paste ingredients in a mortar or simply buying ready-made curry pastes in tiny cans, jars, or plastic pouches. Curiously, *shitor din*, a spicy paste from West Africa, is almost exactly the same as the base of these Thai pastes: dried shrimp and chiles pounded in oil. Also, as in Thailand, ready-mixed *shito* is available in markets for urban cooks who lack the time and mortar needed to make the traditional sauce for themselves. Alternatively, they can prepare a fresh version, with the same name but more like a salsa, using chiles, tomatoes, and onions.

The *nam phriks* of Thailand are pounded chile and fermented-fish sauces, much like *sambals*. Their viscosity varies, from sauces as thin as Tabasco to pastes that are nearly dry. Also like *sambals*, they come in dozens of local varieties.

"Chili sauce" refers to certain *sambals* that may or may not be hot. They shouldn't be confused with bottled American "chili sauce," which is merely a variation on ketchup—albeit one that may be slightly spicy. According to the USDA's definition, chili sauces may contain at least some green or red peppers, but it's not a requirement.

Asian chile sauces, by contrast, are made primarily of peppers, either hot or sweet. Thai sweet chili sauce, for example, consists of bits of pickled chiles suspended in a slightly jellied solution of vinegar and several forms of sugar, colored with paprika. It can be used as an ingredient (as a glaze) or a condiment or dipping sauce. It's like generic Chinese duck sauce, but with attitude.

Chinese hot chili paste, *la jiao jiang*, is only used as an ingredient—though a dollop of it may be served atop a dish, to be stirred in by the diner, at the table. It's almost entirely chile pepper, fermented with garlic and sometimes soybeans, then ground coarsely in oil. One exception—in

Nineteenth-century label for a chili sauce bottle. *Source:* Public domain

which hot chili paste comes to the table directly, unalloyed by other ingredients—comes to mind: *Dan dan* noodles (fresh noodles, served cold, with an emulsified sauce of sesame paste and/or peanut butter, sesame oil, Sichuan peppercorns, minced garlic and ginger, soy sauce, and sugar) are often garnished with cucumber, sliced chicken, scallions, and a contrasting spoonful of glistening red *la jiao jiang*. All or some of that spicy paste, depending on the diner's tolerance for pain, gets stirred into the noodles at table.

The familiar Thai (and other Southeast Asian) peanut sauce that typically accompanies grilled skewers of chicken (*saté*) is served hot. The peanut butter is thinned with lime juice and soy and sweetened with jaggery or brown sugar. Like the sauce for the sesame noodles, it's loaded with minced garlic and ginger, but with Thai chile paste instead of Chinese hot pepper paste. It tastes more Southeast Asian because it's thinned with fish sauce and gets a sour kick from tamarind or lime juice.

Salsa de cachuate y chile de árbol is oddly reminiscent of these peanut sauces, though it has a decidedly Mexican twist. Dried árbol chiles and black pepper replace the hot pepper paste, and spices (allspice and thyme) reflect

Chinese chili paste with garlic, an intense addition to Sichuan sauces, such as that on Mapo Tofu. *Source:* Gary Allen

the tropical flavors of Chiapas. It differs from the sauce on *dan dan* noodles by being cooked, more like *saté* sauce. Mexican cooks dollop it on grilled chicken or shrimp. *Salsa macha*—a similar Mexican sauce from Veracruz—is an uncooked purée of peanuts with dried chiles, garlic, and olive oil.

Ethiopians make a paste of their spice blend, *berbere* ("composed of hot and sweet Chiles, it also contains a great, and varying, number of other herbs and spices, such as Allspice, Basil, Bishop's Weed, Black Pepper, Cardamom, Cinnamon, Cloves, Coriander, Cumin, Fenugreek leaves and seeds, Garlic, Ginger, Onions, Nutmeg, Rue Seeds, Salt and Turmeric"[17]). The ingredients are pounded together with garlic, then moistened with wine. The resulting paste, called *awaze*, is used as a dip or condiment at table.

Ketchup has occasionally been called "red sauce" (especially in countries of the British Commonwealth), but most people would agree that this term more often applies to Italian tomato sauce—the stuff we find on spaghetti and pizza. We know that the French have their *sauce tomate*, but Italian red sauces are more iconic. What distinguished the Italian red sauces from their French relatives is the fact that *sauce tomate* is thickened with roux, whereas Italian sauces achieve their viscosity by reduction—that is, they increase the relative amount of suspended matter by eliminating some of the suspending liquid.

In Louisiana, "tomato gravy" is similar to *sauce tomate*, though it usually contains green peppers, onions, and some form of cured pork fat. Sometimes called "Creole sauce," or *sauce picante*, it is definitely not the "gravy" or "Sunday gravy" prepared by Italian Americans. That garlic-scented tomato sauce is enriched by several meats: braciole, meatballs, sausages, and maybe even pork chops.

Historic Recipe: Vermicelli co le Pomodoro

Pick four rotola . . . of tomatoes. Cut out any blemishes, remove the seeds and water and boil the tomatoes. When they are soft, pass the pulp through a sieve and cook down by a third. When the sauce is sufficiently dense, boil two rotola . . . of vermicelli. Drain the pasta and add it to the sauce along with salt and pepper. Stir and cook the mixture until the sauce has dried and serve.[18]

Ippolito Cavalcanti's recipe, above, from 1839 was the first of a vast continuum of Italian tomato-based sauces—from basic marinara[19] (tomatoes, olive oil, garlic, red pepper, basil, and oregano) to *sugo alla puttanesca* ("whore's sauce"—like marinara but intensified with anchovies, capers, and olives—a relatively modern invention created no earlier than the 1950s in Campania) to *sugo all'amatriciana* (sauce for a woman of Amatrice—like marinara but with added *guanciale*, jowl bacon, and sometimes onion and chile) to *arrabbiata* ("angry" sauce—also like marinara but with even more hot pepper; think *fra diavolo*). Italian red sauces constitute an extended family of daughter sauces on their own.

Ragù, which many consumers only know as a brand of jarred tomato sauce, is etymologically connected to French ragoût,[20] a kind of slow-cooked stew. The Italian American Sunday sauce is basically *ragù alla napoletana*, a thick meat sauce with plenty of tomatoes cooked so long that the various forms of beef, pork, and veal fall apart. *Ragù alla barese* (from Bari, in Apulia) is similar but made with beef, lamb, pork, and even—occasionally—horse. Those southern Italian sauces are very different from *ragù alla sugo alla bolognese* and *ragù alla genovese*. The former uses very little tomato product and the latter none at all, being mostly chunks of beef simmered with onions. Rich *ragù di fegatini*, a specialty of Emilia Romagna, is chopped chicken livers slowly cooked in butter, with milk and chicken stock, seasoned with bay leaf and freshly ground nutmeg. This *ragù* is served atop tagliatelle that has been sauced with egg yolks and grated Parmigiano-Reggiano. It's much like carbonara, minus the black pepper and *guanciale*. Unlike French *ragoûts*, Italian *ragùs* are served not on their own but as sauces for pasta.

Some tomato sauces are uncooked. *Checca* sauce is a summery mix of minced fresh tomatoes, olive oil, and basil, with morsels of mozzarella, that serves as a topping for hot pasta. It's something like *insalata caprese* and pasta, all in one bowl. I sometimes make this sauce when tomatoes and herbs are at their best:

Recipe: Summer Sauce

Yield: enough sauce for a pound of pasta

Ingredients

3	large ripe tomatoes, coarsely chopped
1	shallot, peeled and coarsely chopped
1 Tbsp.	extra virgin olive oil
1 Tbsp.	fresh tarragon, chopped
to taste	salt and freshly ground black pepper

Method

1. Place first four ingredients in blender or food processor. Blend until not quite smooth, with some small chunks still visible.
2. Adjust seasoning with salt and pepper.
3. Allow to rest, covered, for at least a half-hour, so flavors can blend.
4. Toss with hot pasta.

Of course, the Italians couldn't have had tomatoes until after the New World was discovered—and they only learned to make tomato sauce from the Spanish, who had in turn learned about it in Mexico. Bernardino de Sahagún, a Franciscan missionary to the New World, had seen Aztecs preparing it in the mid-sixteenth century. Mexicans still make a descendant of that ancient sauce: *salsa de tomate rojo*. It's tomatoes (fresh or canned) cooked with olive oil, salt, sugar, and ground *chile negro*.

Italians did have at least one red sauce, even before the introduction of the New World's *pomodoro*. In the fourteenth century, a merchant, Francesco Datini, traveled between Avignon, Florence, and Venice. He chronicled every aspect of his life in hundreds of thousands of documents (that were only discovered in the nineteenth century), and among them he listed a particular favorite dish: *savore sanguino*, a blood-colored sauce made of minced meat, wine, and a pounded mixture of fragrant red sandalwood, cinnamon, raisins, and sumac. Think of it as a kind of Middle Eastern *ragú bolognese*.

Once adopted in Italy, tomato sauce traveled and evolved around the Mediterranean. Greek and Balkan recipes often include cinnamon and honey (which is why Cincinnati chili has a sweetly spicy taste—the first makers of that regional dish all emigrated from the Balkans). Rochester sauce, from upstate New York, tops hot dogs. Like Cincinnati chili, it's a ground meat sauce with onion and garlic, sweetened with allspice, cinnamon, and cloves, but it actually contains some chili powder. Chili dogs, New York City style, are topped with a sauce that's closer to *chili con carne*, containing chile powder, cumin, oregano, ground beef, and some tomato product. The secret—the element that makes New York's chili dogs taste different from those from anywhere else—is that the sauce is thinned with the water in which the dogs have cooked for ages. As one wag quipped, "You know Spring has come to New York when the hot dog vendors change the water in their carts."

Dakkous al-tamat, a type of tomato sauce made in Arabic kitchens, is similar to marinara but gets a Middle Eastern edge from lemon juice and cumin. A Lebanese variation contains mint, while one from Kuwait omits herbs but increases the amount of hot pepper. Iraqi cooks might add *baharat* (a variable spice blend consisting of some combination of allspice, black pepper, cardamom, cinnamon, cloves, cumin, hot pepper, and nutmeg).

Arabic cooking techniques influenced European cooking from the days of the Crusades through the Renaissance. Dishes tended to have lots of sweet spices and were thickened with ground nuts. The Spanish brought that tradition to Mexico, where they discovered that the Aztecs were already doing similar things with their sauces. Moles (like the famous *mole poblano*) and *pipians*, which used ground pumpkin seeds instead of nuts, were much like the Islamic sauces the conquistadors already knew.

The mole idea returned to the Iberian Peninsula (at least the chile part). The classic Catalan sauce, *romesco*, pounds roasted red peppers, both sweet and hot, with garlic and oil, thickened with breadcrumbs and, in true Islamic fashion, nuts (usually almonds but, at times, hazelnuts or pine nuts).

Recipe: Romesco Sauce I

Ingredients

1	dried sweet or slightly hot large red pepper such as "New Mexico" style, seeds and stems removed
½	dried red chili pepper, seeds removed
1 cup	water
½ cup	red wine vinegar
¾ cup	olive oil
2 slices	French-style bread, ¼ inch thick
1	large tomato, skinned and chopped
36	blanched almonds (about two ounces), lightly toasted
6 cloves	garlic, peeled and chopped
to taste	salt

Method

1. Place the dried pepper and chili pepper in a saucepan with the water and vinegar. Bring to a boil, then simmer 5 minutes. Drain and cool.
2. In a skillet, heat ¼ cup of the oil. Fry the bread slices until golden on both sides. Remove.

3. In the same oil sauté the tomato for about 3 minutes.

4. Place the peppers, fried bread, tomatoes (including the oil in which they were cooked), almonds, garlic, the remaining ½ cup of oil, and the salt in a processor or blender, until well blended but with small pieces remaining.

5. Let sit at room temperature until ready to use.[21]

Xató differs somewhat from *romesco*; it replaces almonds with hazelnuts, is sharpened with lemon juice, and uses only *nyora* peppers (the ones used to produce Spanish paprika). *Salvitxada*, another *romesco* variant, doesn't grind nuts to thicken it. Garlic-rubbed toast and a little vinegar perform that function.

The Islamic influence had also spread through central Africa, where after New World squashes and pumpkins were introduced, their seeds were pounded into a kind of flour (*egusi*) that thickened soups into sauces. These *pipian*-like *egusi* sauces are still common in Africa and often include chiles, onions, tomatoes, and palm oil. A thinner version, still called *egusi*, is more of a soup.

Korean fish sauces tend to be cloudy, with suspended particles of fermented fish, so they're not included in the "Solutions" chapter. *Aekjeot*, like Japanese fish sauces, can be made from many different fish species. Anchovies (*myoelchi*) are the most common, but similar sauces can be fermented from shrimp (*saewoojeot*) or various sand lances, known as *kanari* (*Ammodytes* ssp.) as well.

Brazilian *tucupi* is prepared from cassava tubers (*Manihot esculenta*) by pressing and allowing the starch, known as manioc or tapioca, to settle out. Since cassava contains two glycosides that are broken down by the enzyme linamarase to produce poisonous hydrogen cyanide, *tucupi* must be boiled for a long time before it becomes safe to consume. The cloudy yellow sauce is sour and is commonly used with fatty meats, such as duck.

Speaking of duck, already rich *sauce bordelaise* is sometimes made even richer by stirring in the puréed blood, liver, and marrow of the duck. That extravagant suspension is called *sauce rouennaise* and accompanies the remaining part of a pressed duck. It's a rather old-fashioned recipe, one that's not seen very often anymore, except in the fanciest (old-school) French white-tablecloth establishments.

The most rarified forms of suspension sauces are probably foams and smokes. Foam is merely a mass of bubbles of gas suspended in a liquid.

Whipped cream is a typical example; tiny pockets of air (or, in the case of aerosol canned whipped cream, nitrous oxide gas) are distributed throughout a matrix composed of butterfat and milk proteins. Thousands of tiny gas bubbles disrupt the liquid's flow, making it more viscous, or thicker. As long as the foam is kept cold enough to prevent the butterfat from melting and allowing trapped gas to escape, it is fairly stable. The bubbles in less viscous foams are supported only by the surface tension of the liquid; they are considerably more ephemeral.

Nondairy whipped toppings are an amalgam of industrial products: emulsifiers, partially hydrogenated oil, stabilizers, sweeteners (corn syrup, high-fructose corn syrup, and/or nonnutritive substances like aspartame and neotame), and water. Fat-free varieties substitute various gums for the oil. Strangely, one brand of nondairy topping (Cool Whip) outsells real whipped cream (such as Reddi-wip) by a wide margin.[22]

Sweet whipped cream recipes have been around at least since the sixteenth century. This anonymous one features an ingredient that is fairly exotic to modern Western tastes but was common in medieval Europe and still appears in recipes from the Middle East: rosewater.

Historic Recipe: A Dyschefull of Snowe

Take a pottelle of swete thycke creame and the whytes of eyghte egges, and beat them altogether wyth a spone, then putte them in youre creame and a saucerfull of Rosewater, and a dyshe full of Sugar wyth all, then take a stycke and make it cleane, and than cutte it in the end foure square, and therewith beate al the aforesayde thynges together and ever as it ryseth take it of and put it in a Collaunder. . . . And yf you have wafers caste some wyth all and thus serve them forthe.[23]

Foams, such as whipped cream, don't have to be sweet (the dessert version is *crème Chantilly*). They can be flavored with mint, lemon zest, or horseradish (or wasabi) as savory sauces for cold dishes—the last two make delightful adjuncts to smoked trout. The only connection between *crème Chantilly* and *sauce Chantilly* (a hollandaise derivative) is that both include whipped cream. *Chantilly* is another name for *mousseline*, a sauce lightened by foam, be it whipped cream or stiffly beaten egg whites.

Another dessert, zabaglione, is usually prepared tableside because its warm foam of egg yolks and sugar, flavored with marsala wine, is fairly unstable. More solid and stable egg foams, such as meringues and soufflés, manage to maintain their structure only through complete cooking of their proteins—their essential protein being albumen, which is found only in the whites of the eggs. Zabaglione can never be firmer than a soft custard because, while yolks do contain proteins, albumen is not one of them—which is also why, when they're cooked, their texture is so different.

Many liquids can form foams, but most are rather evanescent. Modern culinary applications for more stable foams require the use of emulsifiers (so will be addressed in the chapter on emulsions). Perhaps the most extreme examples of suspensions are the smokes so beloved by molecular gastronomers. Savory tea leaves, wood chips, or herbs are burned, and their fumes are forced into small balloons of blown sugar or under a glass dome. At the table the guest breaks open the sparkling globe of smoke or whisks away the transparent cloche and inhales the fragrant cloud. It's the purest form of sauce imaginable: it's a fluid saturated with desirable aromas, it enhances the flavor of one's meal (our perception of flavor is, after all, mostly olfactory), it's free of any artificial thickeners, and it's utterly devoid of calories. Scented smokes, when output by a device that's rather like a small hair dryer, can also serve as ingredients in other sauces.[24]

We can consider smokes sauces since they are fluid, often a by-product of the cooking process, and serve to enhance the dishes they accompany. They consist of microscopic particles or droplets (of the foodstuff being served, the cooking medium, or the fuel used for cooking, or else some combination of these) suspended in the air. Obviously these particles tend to disperse throughout the room, so they must be contained until served with a flourish at the table. They are also likely to fall out of suspension if they cool (hot air molecules move much more energetically than cool ones, and it's the bumping around by all that movement that keeps the smoke particles from settling out, or condensing).

Are the smokes of molecular gastronomers really all that different from the fragrant essence of ortolan ostentatiously—if surreptitiously—inhaled by gourmets? Only, perhaps, in their delivery system.

Suspensions, by their very nature, are temporary—unless aided by exterior forces (or compounds). However, some interesting variations on the suspension theme will be addressed in the following chapters—beginning with the next one on gels.

9

GELS

A gel can be thought of as a special, reverse sort of suspension in which relatively small amounts of starch or protein swell with absorbed liquid. In effect, the liquid is suspended in a matrix of these other substances. If made well, gel-based sauces that build upon simple solutions are appetizingly transparent but thick enough to feel rich and substantial.

While most proteins, when cooked, become more solid (think of the white of an egg or raw chicken flesh), some proteins are soluble under certain conditions. Specifically, the collagen that forms connective tissue in bones, skin, and ligaments—if cooked long and at a simmering temperature—will release gelatin into an aqueous solution. Individual molecules of protein drift as tiny strands throughout the liquid. As water is removed through evaporation, some of the strands connect to one another, forming a three-dimensional network that stabilizes the liquid, preventing it from flowing freely. The liquid becomes more viscous. If the resulting gelatin solution is further reduced (bringing the strands into even closer contact), a gel forms that is solid at room temperature (such as *glace de viande*, aspic, or Jell-O).

A culinarily useful feature of such gels is that they melt when reheated. The increased movement of the liquid's molecules (that's all heat is) pushes the strands apart, and the *glace* melts. Chunks of solidified *glace*, when added to other liquids, melt, giving them increased viscosity and a rich mouth-feel. If one of these collagen-thickened sauces becomes too thick upon cooling, its viscosity can be adjusted merely by reheating or adding water.

Bartolomeo Scappi considered gelatin a sauce because ingredients (such as chunks of meat in headcheese or souse) were suspended in it. To our minds, that seems like a rather extreme example—though the warmth of the diner's mouth does melt the gelatin matrix into an unctuous kind of sauce.

Starches also thicken sauces by suspending their liquid components, but they do so in a different manner. Starch granules, when heated in the presence of water, become engorged with it (plus any flavor molecules that happen to be dissolved in it). Think of them as tiny sponges. They immobilize the water, preventing it from flowing. This increases the liquid's viscosity to different degrees, depending on the starch-to-water ratio, the type of starch, and the degree to which the resulting gel is allowed to cool.

Some gelatinized starches yield sauces that are transparent, or nearly transparent, as seen in many Chinese dishes, especially those made outside China.

Hoisin sauce—ground chiles, garlic, and soybeans, suspended in a sugar solution (the version from Beijing uses some vinegar)—is thickened with various starch gels derived from rice and/or wheat. It is an ingredient in many Chinese sauces but is also served as a condiment in its own right. It is frequently combined with other ingredients to make dips, and not just in Chinese cooking. The Vietnamese call it *tuong den* and serve it with southern-style *phở* and spring rolls. *Tianmianjiang*, sweet bean sauce, is very similar to hoisin (and is often used in its place) but is a little sweeter. In Korea, the same sauce is known as *chunjang*.

Hoisin's name (Cantonese for "seafood") suggests that it should be used with fish, but most Westerners are more familiar with it as the sweet companion to Peking duck. Many prepared Chinese sauces, such as lobster sauce and duck sauce, receive their names from their intended use, not their main ingredient. Pale lobster sauce lacks soy sauce and is basically starch-thickened chicken stock flavored with garlic, ginger, and sometimes a garnish of fermented black beans. Duck sauce—so often found in little plastic pouches at the bottom of a takeout bag—is a thin jelly of apricots, peaches, plums, or pineapples, plus ginger, chile, sugar, and vinegar. When intended to serve as an ingredient instead of a condiment, it's sold in jars labeled "plum sauce."

Oyster sauce, however, is actually made of oysters (with the exception of vegetarian oyster sauce, which gets its umami from mushrooms). It also contains salt, sugar, and hydrolyzed vegetable protein—a soy sauce surrogate. Starch, usually in the form of wheat flour, provides its viscosity; consequently its soft gel is cloudy, not transparent.

Most Filipino dipping sauces are quite thin and uncooked—just a sour liquid with various garnishes. However, that cuisine's sweet-and-sour sauce, made to accompany fried appetizers, is a solution of brown sugar, soy sauce, and vinegar (or *kalamansi* juice) heated to thicken with tomato-based ketchup and a slurry of either corn starch or flour. Filipinos also cook a plum sauce that contains cayenne, preserves, and vinegar—in a thin gel of corn starch.

While many of his sauces depended on flour for thickening, Auguste Escoffier recognized the value, and potential, of other starches. "Starch being the only one from among the different constituents of flour which really affects the thickening of sauces, there would be considerable advantage in preparing *roux* either from a pure form of it, or from substances with kindred properties, such as . . . arrowroot, corn starch, etc. It is only habit that causes flour to be still used as the binding element of *roux*, and, indeed, the hour is not so far distant when the advantages of the changes I propose will be better understood."[1] While the largely starch-based sauce hierarchy of Escoffier may no longer adequately describe today's much more eclectic collection of sauces, a few classicists lament the loss of the old ways. André Soltner, one of the last practitioners of classic French cuisine, was quite outspoken on the subject: "I am worried because in the past ten years, we have gotten away from these sauces. This has happened before. Forty years ago, when nouvelle cuisine was in vogue, chefs thought that roux-thickened sauces were too heavy. They tried to thicken sauces with purées or arrowroot or just butter. I think they were wrong, but we're seeing it again. The younger generation of chefs doesn't know how to make them. If they haven't learned, they might be able to cook nicely—but they will not be able to cook properly."[2]

Starch-thickened sauces are truly ancient. The "cereal cake" used as a thickener in Mesopotamia served essentially the same function as ship's biscuit used to thicken chowders or the ginger snap cookie crumbs that convert sauerbraten's marinade into the gravy that joins it at the table.

A common complaint about starch-thickened sauces (especially gravies) is their tendency to form unpalatable lumps. Lumps can easily be avoided if we think about the way starches behave when added to hot aqueous solutions.

If you were to fish a typical lump out of a sauce and slice it in half, its structure would be obvious. The outside of the lump is moist and shiny, while the inside consists of dry, unmixed starch. The structure reveals the lump's formation. When starches are mixed with hot water (usually around 141 degrees Fahrenheit, depending on the type of starch), the individual grains swell as they absorb water. The process is known as gelatinization. Gelatinized starch is relatively impermeable, which is to say it doesn't allow water to pass through it. When hot water is added too quickly, the outside of a small mass of dry starch gelatinizes, sealing and preventing water from reaching the raw starch inside. A lump is born.

If, however, you mix the starch into cold water to form a slurry (so no gelatinization occurs) and then add it to the hot water, each individual granule is gelatinized, and a nice smooth sauce is the result. This method succeeds because the starch granules are kept separate until they are heated to the point of gelatinization.

Other methods accomplish the same result. French chefs stir *beurre manié* into hot stock to thicken sauces. *Beurre manié* is merely a mixture of flour and butter, rubbed together—literally in one's hand—effectively coating each tiny grain in a layer of fat. That way, hot liquid never has a chance to coat a mass of starch with impermeable gel. Its primary advantage over roux is that it requires no separate cooking and can adjust a sauce's viscosity at the last minute. Small bits of *beurre manié* are simply tossed into the cooking liquid and stirred until it's properly thickened.

The roux in classic French sauces does the same thing but uses hot fat, instead of cold butter, to isolate the particles of flour and cook out some of their raw taste. In the seventeenth century, François Pierre La Varenne laid out the proper way to use roux to thicken sauces.

Historic Recipe: Thickening of Flowre

Melt some lard, take out the mammocks;[3] put your flowre into your melted lard, seeth it well, but have a care it stick not to the pan, mix some onion with it proportionably. When it is enough, put all with good broth, mushrums and a drop of vinegar. Then after it hath boiled with its seasoning, pass all through the strainer and put it in a pot. When you will use it, you shall set it upon warm embers for to thicken or allay your sauces.[4]

French cooks recognize three stages of roux browning: white (in which the flour is cooked, without color, in clarified butter), blond (cooked in butter until it's a pale golden color), and brown (cooked in butter or other fat until light brown). In Louisiana, Cajun cooks have a fourth category; their dark brown roux is much darker than their French forebears would ever make. Cajun roux has a very different flavor (because of complex Maillard reactions that are possible because the use of oil permits higher temperatures than butter), but it also has reduced thickening power. That's because the extended cooking time breaks much of the starch into simple sugars, which are then turned into a host of different compounds, none of which form gels. As a rule, the darker the roux, the more that is needed to achieve the same viscosity as can be obtained from a lighter roux.

A simple starch-thickened example, from continental French cuisine, is *sauce poivrade*. Flour is stirred into hot mirepoix, much as one would do in making gumbo, but wine (and a little vinegar) moistens the mass, to which a lot of black pepper is added. This should not be confused with the sauce for *steak au poivre*. In that case, steak, heavily crusted with coarse black pepper, is sautéed and removed from the pan, in which chopped shallots are cooked; then the pan is deglazed with a bit of brandy, and butter is stirred in at the end (consequently, the sauce for *steak au poivre* is not a gel; it's an emulsion).

Cooks in Louisiana have other thickeners in their arsenal beyond the various shades of roux; okra provides additional polysaccharide-enhanced viscosity when cooked in aqueous foods. Some gumbos use *filé* powder (derived from leaves and cambium of Sassafras trees, *Sassafras albidum*) to "tighten" their sauce. It had been used as a thickener by indigenous Native Americans long before the Cajuns arrived. Note Miss Leslie's charming spelling error in this mid-nineteenth-century recipe:

Historic Recipe: Filet Gumbo

Cut up a pair of fine plump fowls into pieces, as when carving. Lay them in a pan of cold water, till all the blood is drawn out. Put into a pot, two large table-spoonfuls of lard, and set it over the fire. When the lard has come to a boil, put in the chickens with an onion finely minced. Dredge them well with flour, and season slightly with salt and pepper; and, if you like it, a little chopped marjoram. Pour on it two quarts of boiling water. Cover it, and let it simmer slowly for three hours. Then stir into it two heaped tea-spoonfuls of sassafras powder. Afterwards, let it stew five or six minutes longer, and then send it to table in a deep dish; having a dish of boiled rice to be eaten with it by those who like rice.

This gumbo will be much improved by stewing with it three or four thin slices of cold boiled ham, in which case omit the salt in the seasoning. Whenever cold ham is an ingredient in any dish, no other salt is required.

A dozen fresh oysters and their liquor, added to the stew about half an hour before it is taken up, will also be an improvement.

If you cannot conveniently obtain sassafras-powder, stir the gumbo frequently with a stick of sassafras root.

This is a genuine southern receipt. Filet gumbo may be made of any sort of poultry, or of veal, lamb, venison, or kid.[5]

In the United States, we have two distinct types of "gravy." Italian Americans, especially those who live on the East Coast and trace their ancestry to Sicily, make a sauce they call "gravy," but it is actually a tomato sauce, usually enriched by several different meats and often served on weekends or holidays. That is not the kind of gravy we're discussing at the moment. In America, most of the sauces we call "gravy" are starch thickened, though the preferred forms of starch (it's not *always* flour), liquid, garnish, and fat vary considerably from region to region.

Most gravies are based on flour that is browned in residual cooking fat, then combined with water or stock. They are commonly garnished with mushrooms or giblets (bits of cooked liver from the chicken or turkey the gravy will accompany). There are, naturally, a great many exceptions to that pattern.

Southern red-eye gravy, served with country ham, is made by stirring flour into the fat that is left in the skillet after frying the ham. Once the flour has cooked, the pan is deglazed with leftover coffee, plus a little brown sugar to temper the bitter coffee and salty fried ham. In Louisiana, a variation of red-eye gravy is made with slow-cooked beef, and the coffee will, as likely as not, contain chicory. A Texan variant of Louisiana red-eye might be sweetened with honey instead of brown sugar and brightened with lime juice and chile.

Some regional gravies use milk as the fluid component. The most unusual one, said to have been a favorite of Elvis Presley,[6] is chocolate gravy.

Cook cocoa powder and flour in milk (rather like a thin pudding), and then enrich with butter and garnish with crumbled cooked bacon. First created in the Appalachian Mountains and the hills of the Ozarks, this unlikely mélange is poured over hot buttermilk biscuits.

When Texans pan-fry pounded and breaded pieces of beef to make their beloved chicken-fried steaks, they'll add flour and lots of black pepper to the crust that is left in the pan, then stir in milk to make a white—"cream"—gravy. Southern fried chicken is sometimes served with a similar gravy made with the residue of chicken fat and crispy bits of breading left in the pan. No diner or truck stop in the South could hope to stay in business if it didn't offer a breakfast (served twenty-four hours a day) of biscuits smothered in a milk-based gravy made in the pan used to fry country sausage. It must be redolent of sage and black pepper and studded with little bits of browned forcemeat. Added cayenne pepper makes this sausage gravy (also known as sawmill gravy) spicier. In northern Georgia, a local variant of sausage gravy employs both bacon and sausage. This darker sauce is called "combination gravy." Individual cooks vary basic sausage gravy by substituting heavy cream for milk or adding Worcestershire sauce or Tabasco. New Englanders make their milk gravy by substituting salt pork for sausage. Midwestern milk gravy replaces the meats listed above with ground beef and might be "beefed up" with bottled steak sauce—A.1. or Worcestershire—and/or beef bouillon.

In parts of the South, bacon drippings provide the fat for gravy, which might be made with buttermilk or sweet milk, but occasionally ordinary flour is replaced with cornmeal as the thickener. This sauce verges on gruel and is sometimes served as a dish on its own—rather than as an accompaniment. A Texan take on cornmeal-thickened gravy might start with lard, then add masa (finely ground hominy, normally used to make tortillas and tamales) and the kinds of spices one would expect in *chili con carne*—chili powder, cumin, garlic, and oregano—moistened with enough chicken stock to reach the desired consistency.[7]

Much further north, across the Canadian border in fact, light brown gravy—homemade, or straight from a jar, or even made with powdered gravy mix—plays a starring *rôle* in the traditional (if not quite national) dish: *poutine*. Beginning in francophone Canada (but now found almost throughout the country), plates of *pommes frites*—French fries—are topped with hot gravy and cheese curds. There were, at one time, many types of *poutine* in Quebec, but the term is now reserved for the iconic fries-gravy-cheese-curd dish. There are many hypotheses about the etymology of the dish's name, but I suspect that it is a snide reference to a traditional—and more expensive—dish from the Mediterranean Côte d'Azur. *La poutine* is baby anchovies or sardines crisply fried into something that resembles the much cheaper fried potatoes of Canada. The potato-gravy-cheese-curd dish has spawned countless variations in Canada and around the world.

One of them, from English-speaking Ottawa, is an affront to the quint-essentially British sweet-savory distinction. Sugar shack *poutine* tops the basic dish with bacon, maple syrup, and sausage. Another—perhaps the most linguistically incomprehensible—variation comes from Quebec itself: *poutine Chinoise* (literally, "Chinese poutine"), a plate of fries smothered in a mixture of brown gravy and *ragù bolognese*.

Commercial canned gravy comes in two basic forms: a brown one, labeled "beef," and a yellowish one, called "chicken." Both are likely thickened with modified food starch instead of flour. Modified starch uses a number of chemicals, such as aluminum sulfate (alum) and/or sodium hydroxide (lye, used to pre-gelatinize starch[8]), among others. The flavor of these canned sauces usually has its umami-factor boosted by monosodium glutamate (MSG), and artificial colorings and flavorings are likely among their ingredients. None of these compounds, used in moderation, is harmful. However, reading the labels on the cans is likely to adversely affect one's appetite.

Some spices work like flour to thicken sauces; the individual particles swell by absorbing some of the surrounding liquid. Ground dried chiles thicken moles (though ground nuts, seeds, and even bits of tortillas are certainly involved as well), in part because their particles absorb liquid but also because they contain gel-producing pectin. "Fenugreek seeds exude a gum that gives a gelatinous consistency"[9] to dishes that incorporate curry powder.

The word "pectin" is derived from a Greek word meaning "clotted" or "congealed," which is hardly appetizing to modern ears. This is especially ironic since pectin-thickened solutions are often perfectly transparent, yielding clear and richly colored sauces.

Pectin is a compound that occurs naturally in the cell walls of various fruits. It stiffens the cell walls and binds the cells together, creating a firm or crisp texture. As fruit ripens, the enzyme pectinase gradually breaks down the pectin (in overripening, the process has gone too far, making the fruit unpleasantly soft and mushy). When pectin-rich fruits (especially if slightly underripe) are cooked, molecules of sugar-like substances (saccharides) link themselves into long chains (polymers), forming a gel. Citrus marmalades and canned cranberry sauce are perfect examples of jellies whose viscosity has been enhanced by the presence of pectin.

Such jellies are sometimes served as condiments, or they can be added to pan sauces, instead of starch or butter, to thicken and add flavor. Red currant jelly, for example, is often used in pan sauces for roasted meats: goose, lamb, turkey, or venison. Its tart flavor complements, or civilizes, the sometimes gamy flavor of the aged meat. The sauce is made by melting the jelly together with mustard and/or rosemary. Variations—such as Cumberland sauce or Oxford sauce—might be thinned with port. Americans' cranberry jelly as a companion to turkey is probably an adaptation of red currant jelly, using more readily available New World fruit. Homemade cranberry sauce, made with berries, sugar, orange juice and zest, and typical medieval sweet spices (allspice, cinnamon, clove), thickens as it cooks due to pectin that is naturally present in the berries.

Cranberry sauce and the mint jelly often served with lamb are sweet-savory combinations that are throwbacks to medieval culinary practices. They tend to be served on special occasions, like holiday dinners, when old traditions control the menu.

What we call "starch" is actually two different kinds of starch: amylose and amylopectin. Amylose does not form gels when cooked, but amylopectin does (as the "pectin" part of the name suggests). Depending on its source, the "starch" might contain one or both in varying proportions, which affects its properties. Rice, for example, contains both, but different varieties have them in different proportions. Short-grain rices (like arborio or carnaroli) are largely composed of amylopectin, so they produce the creamy sauce in risottos. Long-grain rices are mostly composed of amylose, so they are not sticky when cooked; they could be used to thicken a sauce but only in the way a purée acts (increasing viscosity with suspended particles). Such sauces will not be as smooth or translucent as those made with short-grain rice.

Other starches employed as thickeners for sauces include arrowroot, corn, kudzu, potato, tapioca, and wheat.

Nineteenth-century label for a can of jellied cranberries. *Source:* Public domain

Arrowroot powder is extracted from the rhizomes (nontuberous, usually horizontal, swellings of the rootstocks) of various species of tropical plants. West Indian arrowroot (*Maranta arundinacea*) is the main source, but many other plants yield similar starch and have similar names. As it contains no gluten, it is kosher and suitable for those who suffer from celiac disease. It forms gels that are more transparent than those provided by corn starch.

Corn starch yields an inexpensive translucent gel when combined with water in a slurry then heated. In 1837, Alfred Bird created an eggless custard substitute using corn starch and milk. Its use is so widespread that many in England (and the former British colonies) don't even know that true custards contain egg proteins.

Kudzu starch, also known as Japanese arrowroot, forms stronger gels than most other starches, so little is needed to thicken a sauce; a concentration of less than 7 percent is sufficient. Kudzu gels are shiny, translucent, and almost transparent, which makes for a nice presentation in Chinese sauces. The only drawback is that kudzu starch is more expensive than competing starches, like those from corn or arrowroot.

Potato starch has some useful properties; it remains clear through long cooking, which means commercial sauces that must be subjected to high canning temperatures will still look good (that's why it appears in the ingredient lists on so many labels). Like arrowroot, it is an acceptable replacement for wheat in special diets (such as kosher or gluten free).

Tapioca starch, which is washed from the roots of cassava or yucca (*Manihot esculenta*), is sometimes mistakenly identified as arrowroot or as Brazilian arrowroot. It contains 70–85 percent amylopectin, so it forms a transparent gel, but one that doesn't stand up to intense reheating (so it's not used as much as potato starch in commercial applications that require canning).

Wheat starch (as in flour) does create gels, but they're not as strong as those made with corn starch and are considerably less transparent. It is the least expensive form of starch, which is the main reason it is found in so many traditional sauce recipes. Wheat starch is best used in gravies, where opacity is not detrimental. As it's impossible to remove every trace of protein (gluten) in the manufacture of wheat starch, it is not suitable for kosher (Passover) or gluten-free diets.

Unlike gelatin, the gels formed from many starches do not melt evenly when reheated after being cooled. When individual starch grains cook, they break open, and their starch leaks into the solution. When such a sauce cools, the starch molecules crystallize into a form that is less soluble. Reheating generally yields sauces with an uneven texture that most people find unappetizing. Commercial sauces employ a number of additives (and different starches from those available to home cooks) that avoid the problems caused by reheating. Modified food starches, as described above, are among their additives, as are carageenans (there are three varieties, derived from different species of seaweed, each having different properties), which, like pectin, are polysaccharides.

So, the basic principle by which gels add viscosity to liquids is by creating a matrix that slows the movement of water molecules. There are other tools available to the saucier, and the next chapter—on emulsions—looks at one of the most significant methods, albeit a more technically demanding one.

10

EMULSIONS

Suspensions, as we've seen, consist of tiny particles surrounded by liquid, while gels are thickened by having their liquid components trapped inside particles of starch or held together in a matrix of protein. The principle is the same: increase viscosity by interfering with the liquid's freedom of movement, its fluidity.

Emulsions achieve the same thickening in a more sophisticated and correspondingly fragile manner. They combine two liquids that ordinarily don't mix. We often describe incompatible things (or people, or ideas) as being "like water and oil"; yet a merger of the two is exactly what we achieve when we make an emulsion.

Our word "emulsion" is etymologically descended from a seventeenth-century French word, *émulgère* (literally, "to milk out"). Whole milk begins as a natural emulsion of butterfat suspended in whey (a solution of dissolved sugars and salts, with suspended micelles—tiny particles—of the protein casein). However, if left to stand, the cream will separate out (cream has a higher butterfat content), and since—counterintuitively—fat is lighter than water, it rises to the top.[1] In homogenized milk, fat globules have been broken into fragments so tiny that they can't coalesce to form large enough droplets to float to the surface.

Like suspensions, emulsions tend to be opaque, or at least translucent. That's because their tiny droplets of suspended components have different refractive indexes, so they scatter any light that attempts to pass through them. Some emulsions, like milk, are completely white because of they contain suspended casein molecules as well. Nonfat milk looks "thinner"—is not as opaque as whole milk—because its light-scattering fat globules have been removed. It also feels thinner, less viscous, because that emulsified fat isn't there anymore—it's mostly the aqueous phase of milk, practically whey.

Butter, by the way, is not actually a solid; it's a very thick emulsion—but it's the reverse of most other emulsions. A miniscule amount of watery whey is suspended in a matrix of solidified butterfat. The churning process forces the cold fat globules to bump into each other, allowing them to stick together. This traps some of the watery liquid in the tiny spaces between them. The butter is then paddled to squeegee out most of the whey. The tiny amount of water trapped in the butter provides the steam pressure necessary to make puff pastries—or batters containing sugar and butter creamed together—rise as they bake.

A natural emulsion, like cream, can be thickened by carefully heating it. Gradually removing some of the water in the emulsion yields an unctuous sauce, reduced cream, which can be flavored in any number of ways. Remember, however, that emulsions are fragile; if one tries to reduce cream too much, there won't be enough water left to maintain the emulsion, leaving only butterfat (ghee). If you try to reheat a dish that has been sauced with reduced cream, expect to be disappointed; the fat will separate out of the delicate emulsion, and the once creamy white sauce will be nothing but an oily residue of butterfat.

Various peppercorn sauces can be prepared by simmering the pepper in cream as it reduces. Black and green peppercorns are classic, but in the late 1970s pink peppercorns (which are not related to *Piper nigrum* but are the berries of an invasive vine called *Schinus molle*) became briefly fashionable. They lend a faintly mint-like quality to the sauce's piquancy. An experiment with Australian native pepper (*Drimys lanceolata*) created a delicate mauve-colored cream sauce with heat that came on gradually, increasing beyond that of black and white peppers without their faintly resinous aroma.

Any time we wish to make an emulsion, such as mayonnaise or vinaigrette, we beat the mixture to form these tiny globules and disburse one liquid into the other. Sometimes an emulsifier is required to help the process along. A small amount of mustard, for example, aids in emulsifying vinaigrettes and mayonnaise.

Historic Recipe: Fanny Farmer's Mayonnaise Dressing I

Ingredients

1 tsp.	mustard
1 tsp.	salt
1 tsp.	powdered sugar
Few grains	cayenne
2	egg yolks
2 Tbsp.	lemon juice
2 Tbsp.	vinegar
1½ cups	olive oil

Method

Mix dry ingredients, add egg yolks, and when well mixed add one-half tea-spoon of vinegar. Add oil gradually, at first drop by drop, and stir constantly. As mixture thickens, thin with vinegar or lemon juice. Add oil and vinegar or lemon juice alternately, until all is used, stirring or beating constantly. If oil is added too rapidly, dressing will have a curdled appearance. A smooth consistency may be restored by taking yolk of another egg and adding curdled mixture slowly to it. It is desirable to have bowl containing mixture placed in a larger bowl of crushed ice, to which a small quantity of water has been added. Olive oil for making Mayonnaise should always be thoroughly chilled. A silver fork, wire whisk, small wooden spoon, or Dover Egg-beater may be used as preferred. If one has a Keystone Egg-beater, dressing may be made very quickly by its use. Mayonnaise should be stiff enough to hold its shape. It soon liquefies when added to meat or vegetables; therefore it should be added just before serving time.[2]

Lecithin, which is found in egg yolks, works in an ingenious fashion: each molecule of lecithin (or certain other proteins, such as the casein in milk) has different regions that are attracted and attach selectively (based on their electrical charge) to the molecules of water- and oil-based compo-nents. This double nature of lecithin allows it to dissolve as easily in water as in oil. By the way, one reason milk is such a stable emulsion is that all of its casein molecules have the same charge, so they repel each other. Emulsifiers also form thin layers around the fat globules, making it more difficult for them to reconnect.

A basic mayonnaise incorporates three elements: oil, egg yolk, and lemon juice or vinegar. Slowly beating oil into the egg yolk (which is 50% water) and lemon juice (more water), the oil breaks down into tiny droplets that become suspended in the yolk and lemon juice due to the emulsifying agent lecithin in the egg yolk. This phosphorus containing molecule has long "tails" that are lipophilic (fat loving) and hydrophilic (water loving) heads. The tails burrow into the oil and the positive and negatively charged heads attract the water. These, as you might surmise, are the go-between that attracts and firmly binds the water and oil to form the creamy, much-loved sauce.

Mayonnaise can suspend approximately eight times the oil in relation to the water content. At the molecular level it is the tiny oil droplets that are enshrouded in a thin sheen of water that has taken place.[3]

The two liquids in an emulsion are generally described as "phases": the continuous phase, which is usually aqueous, and the dispersed phase, a lipid. The lipid could be oil, as in mayonnaise, or it could be a melted fat, like the butter in hollandaise. In a sense, emulsions are like solutions, but they don't involve dissolvable solutes. Instead, they play on molecular forces to keep bits of insoluble material sufficiently separated so that they can't join together (whereupon their mass would become great enough for gravity to force them to separate).

Stable emulsions can be made when the ratio of dispersed to continuous is about 3:1 (which is why most recipes for vinaigrettes call for that balance; mayonnaise achieves a higher ratio of oil to water because it includes the emulsifier in egg yolks). The Greek version of vinaigrette, *ladolemono*, is much lighter. It's not a salad dressing; it's a quick sauce to pour over grilled seafood, such as *branzino*, octopus, shrimp, or squid. It's both lighter and tarter than other vinaigrettes because it replaces vinegar with lemon juice and uses equal amounts of oil and juice (instead of the usual 3:1 ratio).

In the making of any of these sauces, care must be taken to add the dispersed fat slowly, so that it has a chance to be distributed throughout the water-based liquid. Adding fat too quickly will allow its globules to rejoin, making the sauce "break" into its components rather than form the smooth, thick sauce that we crave.

Many of these freshly made sauces are fragile, temporary things that tend to revert to their original liquids. If they become too hot or too cold, or if they get out of balance—by losing some water through evaporation, for example—they will break (separate into their original components). Mayonnaise, however, is different; it's what is known as a permanent emulsion. The stabilizing effect of its emulsifying agent (the lecithin in the egg yolks) prevents it from breaking. Only if subjected to very high heat, as in cooking, can mayonnaise revert to its oily origins. Vinaigrettes—other than a few heavily stabilized commercial bottled sauces—require frequent shaking or whisking to keep their components from separating.

Since 1933, a mayonnaise-like sauce—which can't legally be called "mayonnaise"[4] because it contains less than the US Department of Agriculture's minimum of 65 percent oil—has divided consumers into the sandwich-making equivalent of the Hatfields and the McCoys. Miracle Whip jars, originally labeled "salad dressing," now say only "dressing"—perhaps to suggest that the sauce can be used in more than just salads. It is produced by Kraft (which also produces the competing Kraft Real Mayonnaise) and was originally intended as a less expensive alternative to mayonnaise. However, many people—especially in the Midwest and Southwest[5]—have come to prefer its sweeter taste, while "real mayonnaise performs better in the Southeast[ern markets]."[6] The "real" mayo is flavored with garlic, onions, paprika, and sugar (none of which would ever be found in French mayonnaise). Miracle Whip is similar but substitutes high-fructose corn syrup for the sugar and maintains the mayo-like texture—despite its reduced fat—with corn starch. The presence of corn starch reveals another difference between mayonnaise and salad dressing: the latter is cooked, while the former is not (if it wasn't cooked, that starch wouldn't gel).

Kraft and competitors (such as Hellmann's/Best) have begun marketing mayonnaise made with olive oil instead of soy oil because customers perceive it as a healthier alternative. These "new" versions of mayonnaise are, in a sense, atavistic, since mayonnaise was originally made with olive oil (which was available in Europe long before soy oil was).

The Japanese have adopted, and adapted, commercial mayonnaise to suit their needs. Kewpie, a leading brand there, employs the same soy oil that is found in Western jarred mayonnaise but changes a few other details. The Japanese only use the yolks, not whole eggs, so their mayo is a deeper yellow. They alter the flavor by adding mirin (making it a little sweeter) and MSG (boosting its umami) and spice it up with a little hot sauce. The now

Trendy mayonnaise jar: it not only uses olive oil but also boasts cage-free eggs—healthy and guilt-free! *Source:* Gary Allen

ubiquitous spicy tuna roll sushi would not exist if mayonnaise had not found its way into Japanese kitchens.

Certain pan sauces, such as *beurre blanc*, make use of butterfat's ability to become creamy when emulsified. An aqueous solution is first made by deglazing the pan with wine, then reducing the liquid to concentrate the meaty flavors from the fond. The fond is the dissolved crust that forms in the bottom of a pan. It is, in essence, a solid mass of flavor formed by the evaporation of meat juices, converted by Maillard reactions into a concentrated layer of umami. Many home cooks hate seeing that crust, thinking only of the additional time they'll have to spend scrubbing it away after dinner. Good cooks love it;

deglazing simultaneously cleans the pan and rescues rich flavor that would otherwise—literally—go down the drain. Once the fond is deglazed with white wine and reduced to just a few tablespoons, chunks of cold butter are whisked in quickly (*monter au beurre*) to thicken and enrich the sauce. *Beurre rouge*, as might be suspected, is the same except for the use of red wine instead of white. These butter sauces tend to separate, but keeping them warm, not hot—in a thermos or surrounded by a hot-water bath known as a bain marie—will extend their lives. Basic *beurre blanc* sauce can be customized by altering the liquid phase (such as by replacing part of the white wine with lemon juice) or adding a garnish (like *tomate concasée*[7]). Such sauces can also be enriched by whisking in a bit of crème fraîche at the last moment.

Sauce bourguignonne is a variant of *beurre rouge*. After meat is sautéed, the pan is deglazed with red wine, together with minced shallots and a bouquet garni of bay leaf, parsley, and thyme tied in a little bundle. The liquid is then strained and reduced. *Sauce espagnole* or a little demi-glace and a sprinkling of cayenne are added next. Finally, cold butter is whisked in to form a luscious emulsion.

Liaison is French for that which binds together, or unifies, disparate ingredients—like oil and water—to form an emulsion. Heavy cream, which is already an emulsion, can be added to produce a liaison (the cream is sometimes beaten together with egg yolks first so the resulting rich liaison has some of the characteristics of a thin custard; *sauce allemande* begins with a velouté made with veal stock). Liaisons can also be made using techniques other than emulsification—such as by creating a suspension of puréed vegetables or lobster roe or thickening by producing a starch-based gel—but only the French could come up with a term that so poetically marries cuisine and romance.

Beurre noisette is butter that has been slowly heated until it separates into butterfat and milk solids. As it heats, the solids begin to brown and form fragrant nutty compounds (hence the *noisette* in the name). At that point, it makes a classic sauce for seafood, especially skate. If the *beurre noisette* is allowed to cook further, it becomes *beurre noir*. At that point, cooking must be stopped, usually by adding lemon juice or vinegar. *Meunière* sauce is *beurre noir* with lemon juice and minced parsley; it becomes *meunière picatta* when capers are added or *amandine* when toasted almonds are the garnish. All of these variations are standard toppings for fried (and breaded) seafood.

As we have seen with zabaglione, carefully heating egg proteins coagulates them, forming custards. "Carefully" is the key concept, because if these proteins are heated too quickly or at too high a temperature, they curdle into insoluble "scrambled eggs," which do not make for an appealing sauce. Examples of egg-thickened sauces include hollandaise (it's the only nonstarch sauce to make it onto Auguste Escoffier's list of mother sauces), Italian carbonara, Italian American Alfredo, and Japanese teppanyaki (which is a gently cooked oil and egg yolk emulsion—sort of a cross between mayonnaise and hollandaise, with an Asian twist).

Cooked egg-based emulsions aren't limited to savory dishes. *Crème anglaise* (flavored with vanilla) and zabaglione (flavored with marsala wine) are fluid cooked custards that serve as dessert sauces—teetering precipitously over the gap between the liquid and solid states. *Crème pâtissière*—the filling for profiteroles, éclairs, and countless other pastries—is basically *crème anglaise* made a bit more viscous by cooking some flour or corn starch in it. Ice cream is merely frozen *crème anglaise*, with air suspended in it by vigorous churning as it freezes. By adding whipped cream to *crème anglaise*, one gets *crème légère* or—by incorporating gelatin—*crème anglaise collée*.

When preparing any of these delicate, custardy sauces, it's essential that temperatures be controlled (between 156°F/70°C and 185°F/85°C), with the highest temperatures resulting in the thickest sauces. However, the risk of producing scrambled eggs, instead of smooth sauce, becomes greater as cooking temperatures rise.

Cooking lemon juice and egg yolks in broth produces Greek *avgolemono* (and similar sauces around the eastern Mediterranean, such as Israeli *agristada*). Greeks and Turks don't agree on much, but their foods share many similarities. Turkish *terbiye*, for example, is much like *avgolemono*.

Among the basic emulsion-based sauces, vinaigrettes are probably the most familiar. They first appeared in English print—appropriately—in John Evelyn's 1699 book *Acetaria: A Discourse of Sallets*. It was a most fitting title, considering the acidic nature of so many salad dressings.

Historic Recipe: Cucumbers in Vinaigrette

20. Cucumber. *Cucumis*; tho' very cold and moist, the most approved *Sallet* alone, or in Composition, of all the *Vinaigrets*, to sharpen the Appetite, and cool the Liver, &c. if rightly prepar'd; that is, by rectifying the vulgar Mistake

of altogether extracting the Juice, in which it should rather be soak'd: Nor ought it to be over *Oyl'd*, too much abating of its grateful *Acidity*, and *palling* the Taste from a contrariety of Particles: Let them therefore be pared, and cut in thin Slices, with a Clove or two of *Onion* to correct the Crudity, macerated in the Juice, often turn'd and moderately drain'd. Others prepare them, by shaking the Slices between two Dishes, and dress them with very little *Oyl*, well beaten, and mingled with the Juice of *Limon*, *Orange*, or *Vinegar*, *Salt* and *Pepper*. Some again, (and indeed the most approv'd) eat them as soon as they are cut, retaining their Liquor, which being exhausted (by the former Method) have nothing remaining in them to help the Concoction. Of old they boil'd the *Cucumber*, and paring off the Rind, eat them with *Oyl*, *Vinegar*, and *Honey*; *Sugar* not being so well known. Lastly, the *Pulp* in Broth is greatly refreshing, and may be mingl'd in most *Sallets*, without the least damage, contrary to the common Opinion; it not being long, since *Cucumber*, however dress'd, was thought fit to be thrown away, being accounted little better than Poyson. *Tavernier* tells us, that in the *Levant*, if a Child cry for something to Eat, they give it a raw *Cucumber* instead of *Bread*. The young ones may be boil'd in White-Wine. The smaller sort (known by the name of *Gerkems*) muriated with the Seeds of *Dill*, and the *Mango* Pickle are for the Winter.[8]

In the 1970s raspberry vinaigrette began to appear on restaurant menus everywhere. To some extent, it's still present. The simplest version is really just raspberry-infused vinegar and oil (plus the usual salt and pepper). A better version—one that qualifies as a composite sauce—uses a purée of fresh berries, two kinds of vinegar (balsamic and cider), mild-flavored oil, some mustard, and a little sugar to counter all that acidity. It's an emulsion and a suspension, plus a few different solutions.

In vinaigrettes and mayonnaise, mustard aids in emulsification, but egg yolks, lecithin, and mustard are not the only emulsifiers that uncooked emulsions utilize. Garlic, if smashed into sufficiently tiny fragments, performs admirably in that role. Accordingly, it is the basis of several garlic sauces from diverse cuisines. Spain's classic aioli is perhaps the simplest. It is nothing but an emulsion of puréed raw garlic and olive oil, pounded together in a mortar and pestle. It needs nothing else, but egg yolk is sometimes added. Garlic-favored mayonnaise may be called "aioli," but, while tasty, it's not true aioli (though I'm certain that Provençal cooks would beg to differ). TV chef Guy Fieri slathers his secret "donkey sauce" on many dishes in his various restaurants. He recently confessed that it's nothing more than an egg-based aioli.[9]

Aioli makes a more grown-up dip for French fries than ketchup, at least if not consumed before going out on a date. Garlic mayonnaise, rendered pink with smoked paprika, is so good with French fries (or roasted wedges of potato) that even the idea of ketchup is easily forgotten. In Egypt and other parts of the Middle East, *toum*—another eggless aioli-like sauce, made with mild sunflower seed oil instead of olive oil—enhances French fries (as well as sandwiches of fried chicken).

Romanian *mujdei*, like aioli, is traditionally made of garlic pounded in oil (though, unlike in Spain, sunflower oil is preferred in Romania). Like aioli, it occasionally includes other ingredients besides oil and garlic; vinegar and cream are common variations. *Mujdei* is served with many foods—fish, meats, and potatoes—and no doubt aids in discouraging visits from vampires.

Elsewhere in the eastern Mediterranean—in what used to be called the Levant—aioli ingredients are pounded with salt and lemon juice (and sometimes mint and/or cayenne) in wooden mortars and pestles to make *toumya*. *Toum* is Arabic for garlic. *Toumya* serves as a dip and a spread for sandwiches (like kebabs, shawarma, or falafel, on pita or similar flatbreads—or just for the bread alone) in Egypt, Iraq, and Lebanon. The emulsion can be maintained merely through the vigorous pounding, but emulsifiers (like egg or lecithin) are sometimes added as well.

Italy's *agliata* is an emulsion of garlic and some vinegar-soaked bread, whipped together with olive oil and thinned with hot chicken stock. The fifteenth-century Martino of Como was a celebrity chef long before Antoine Carême (Bartolomeo Sacchi, aka "Platina," described him as the "prince of cooks from whom I learned all about cooking"). The Eminent Maestro Martino provided this recipe in his *Libro de arte coquinaria*:

Historic Recipe: Agliata Bianca (White Garlic Sauce)

Take well-blanched almonds and grind them, and about halfway through add as much garlic as you like, and grind them well together adding a little cold water so that they don't become oily. Then take a piece of the inside of a loaf of bread and soak it in meat or fish stock, according to the season; and this garlic sauce can be served at any time, as you please.[10]

Recipes for *agliata* in Piemonte add ground almonds or walnuts. The nuts act as emulsifiers for many sauces. The use of ground nuts as emulsifiers to thicken sauces is traditional in ancient Islamic recipes (as well as those of nearby Christian countries, like Greece). Greek *skordaliá* (or *skorthaliá*) beats garlic into oil as well. The Greek version of this sauce differs from the Levantine *toums* by using full-flavored olive oil in place of the milder sunflower oil. *Skordaliá*'s viscosity is often maintained by adding puréed potatoes, ground almonds or walnuts, and even bread (it's the culinary overkill equivalent of wearing a belt *and* suspenders to hold up one's pants).

Tarator is a slightly less garlic-forward sauce found in Albania, Bulgaria, Greece, Macedonia, Lebanon, Syria, and Turkey. Like *skordaliá*, it's mostly an emulsion of ground nuts (walnuts in Turkey, tahini in Lebanon and Syria, though some places replace the tahini with yogurt), olive oil, and lemon juice. It's usually thickened with some breadcrumbs that are first soaked in water. It's almost infinitely variable, with garnishes of cumin, dill, parsley, oregano or other herbs, and even cucumber—which, in yogurt versions, begins to resemble the *tzatziki* of Greece. *Tarators* range in viscosity from thin soups to thicker dips to almost paste-like condiments to be spread on sandwiches.

Georgian *satsivi*—pounded walnuts and garlic emulsified in diluted vinegar—serves as a dip for fried fish and meats. A slightly different version, called *bazhe*, switches pomegranate juice for the vinegar. *Satsivi* and *bazhe* are similar to hummus (except hummus substitutes lemon for vinegar or pomegranate juice, swaps the sesame paste tahini for walnuts, and adds protein in the form of puréed chickpeas). *Maafe* is a spicy West African sauce, thickened by ground peanuts and a little tomato paste (and sometimes puréed sweet potatoes). *Moambe*, the sauce for Congolese *muamba nsusu*, is like *maafe* but includes emulsified palm oil and even more chile. *Bumbu pecel*, a saté-like peanut-butter-thickened sauce from Indonesia, is much spicier than its African cousins. Peanuts and peanut oil are emulsified with ground chiles, *makrut* lime leaves, jaggery, and the ginger-like galangal (*Kaempferia galanga*).

Nuts function as thickeners in a couple of ways: "When nuts are ground into 'butters,' the oil provides the fluid continuous phase that lubricates the particles of cell walls and proteins. But more of the time, nuts are mixed with other ingredients, including liquids, so they become part of a complex suspension and help thicken with both their dry particles and with their oil, which becomes emulsified into tiny droplets."[11]

The fondue-like dipping sauce *bagna cauda* does not contain nuts (though it sometimes includes oils pressed from hazelnuts or walnuts). The hot emulsion is typically formed of olive oil and puréed anchovies and garlic. *Bagna cauda* is a cold-weather alternative to the uncooked dips that are usually served with crudités.

Commercial jarred sauces avoid "separation anxiety" by using chemical emulsifiers and stabilizers (and by adding starches and/or guar gum, locust bean gum, or xanthan gum as thickeners—as will be explained further when we discuss the next category of mother sauces: cultures). Some of these products are also employed by molecular gastronomers (along with a modified soy protein called Versawhip and the colloidal compound methylcellulose F50) to produce stable foams of otherwise impractical liquids. Most of these emulsifiers are used for the standard purpose—allowing oil and water to mix—but one fascinating compound (a monoglyceride emulsifier marketed as Glycerin Flakes) has an additional property: It is only soluble in lipids, not aqueous solutions. Hence, to form a typical emulsion, it is added first to the oil (the reverse of most emulsifying techniques). Still more unusually, it allows lipids to foam. A creative saucier can use it to make a mousse of flavored oil or simply thicken it to sauce consistency without needing to resort to some form of starch.

So we've seen some of the tricks that sauciers have employed to convert flavorful solutions into luxuriously thick sauces. As it turns out, mother nature has already come up with some methods that allow sauces to thicken themselves with practically no effort on the part of the saucier. The next chapter on cultured sauces addresses them.

11

CULTURED SAUCES

We've seen that certain proteins are soluble and can be manipulated with heat to yield gels that thicken liquids into sauces with a rich quality that some have called "mouth-feel." We've also looked at partially dehydrated mixtures, like reduced cream, that move emulsified fat globules closer to each other to create a denser, richer sauce. However, other proteins, those that are not so soluble, can be used to achieve the same richness, albeit by a different means.

The molecules of protein that are suspended in a liquid can be made to change shape and attach themselves together into a viscous matrix by various means. Called denaturing, this process can be caused by heat or by the molecules' chemical environment. Their chemistry could be altered directly by adding an acid (like vinegar or lemon juice) or by allowing some biological activity—fermentation—to create the required acidic environment. Sometimes these methods are used in combination.

The primary source of proteins in cultured products is dairy. The proteins in milk are coagulated by lactobacteria and heat to form yogurts and similar cultured products (commercial buttermilk, for example). Denatured dairy products are the basis of many sauces (though, with the exception of crème fraîche, not in classic French cookery). They are common elsewhere, such as in Indian *raita* and Greek *tzatziki*.

The most basic form of cultured dairy product is soured milk. Milk will naturally go sour on its own, given adequate time, temperature, and the presence of acid-producing bacteria. Various species of lactobacilli—from the genus *Lactococcus* or *Lactobacillus*—feed on sugar (lactose) in the milk and produce lactic acid as a waste product. The lactic acid in turn denatures (curdles) the milk's proteins. The residual acid has a sour flavor, and the denatured proteins thicken the milk. The degree of denaturing and amount of residual moisture determine the viscosity and tartness of the cultured product—ranging from slightly thickened buttermilk to hard cheese.

While milk can be easily soured by biologic activity, it takes some time. Consequently, commercially produced soured milk is usually rushed along with the aid of other acids, among them acetic acid (found in vinegar), hexanedioic acid (found in beets), citric acid (such as lemon juice), fumaric acid (a synthetic substance that also occurs naturally in many fruits), glucodelta lactone (a synthetic acid about one-third as sour as citric acid), hydrochloric acid (much diluted), lactic acid (bypassing the need for bacteria), malic acid (the source of the sour taste in green apples), phosphoric acid (extracted from phosphate rocks and the source of tartness in soft drinks such as colas), succinic acid (found in some fungi but synthesized from acetic acid), and tartaric acid (cream of tartar, originally a by-product of wine fermentation but now mostly synthetic).

Buttermilk was originally the liquid left behind when cultured cream was churned into butter. It was tangy, slightly thickened, and practically fat-free (unless tiny chips of butter were left floating in it). However, most buttermilk today is not a by-product of butter production. It is simply milk that has been inoculated and fermented with lactobacteria—hence it is called "cultured buttermilk." It is thicker, richer, and tangier than old-fashioned buttermilk. Its lactic acid is useful in many culinary applications (such as reacting with baking soda to leaven quick breads or pancakes and marinating meats to tenderize them). Milk soured by any of the acids listed above can be substituted for buttermilk in cooking. Perhaps buttermilk's most familiar role is as the source of thickness and sourness in ranch dressing for salads (though its viscosity is also increased through the incorporation of sour cream, mayonnaise, or yogurt).

Unlike buttermilk, crème fraîche is cultured cream instead of milk. The bacteria used include *Lactococcus cremoris*, *L. lactis*, and *L. lactis* var. *diacetylactis*. The natural product yields a smooth sauce when heated, but low-fat versions (which have their viscosity altered by stabilizing starch or xanthan gum) will not. Full-fat (30 percent) crème fraîche is often used to finish sauces (especially in the cooking of Normandy), providing a rich mouth-feel and mild tartness. It is also added just before serving, as a kind of garnish, to savory dishes and desserts. This function is nearly identical to that of *smetana*, as a garnish for Russian borscht, or *crema*, in Mexican cuisine.

Sour cream is very similar to crème fraîche but usually has a lower fat content (18 to 20 percent), while the low-fat versions are only 14 percent milk fat. The latter are made from a mixture of milk and cream and maintain their viscosity with artificial thickeners, such as carrageenan, gelatin, guar gum, or other starches. Rennet (a collective name for several enzymes derived from the stomach linings of dairy animals, chief of which is chymosin)[1] and/or acids (citric acid or sodium citrate) can be added to assist the bacteria in denaturing the cream's proteins. Sour cream is not as completely fermented as crème fraîche and would spoil easily if not protected by various preservatives (commonly sodium phosphate, sodium citrate, calcium sulfate, and/or potassium sorbate). Sour cream is essential to the cooking of central Europe and Russia—it thickens the sauces in *paprikash* and Stroganoff dishes, as well as some recipes for sauerbraten (though many use crushed gingersnap cookies). Potato dumplings, in northern Germany, are often sauced with *duckefett*, which sounds like "duck fat" but has nothing to do with that luxurious lipid. Instead, it's a mixture of cooked bacon and onions in a sour cream base.

In the United States, sour cream most often appears as a topping for baked potatoes or as an ingredient in dips. The following recipe hardly needs mentioning since it is absurdly easy and has been an American classic since 1952, when a manufacturer of instant soups ran a contest to find new uses for one of its products.

Historic Recipe: Lipton's Onion Dip

Ingredients

2 cups	sour cream
1 package	Lipton's Onion Soup Mix
½ cup	mayonnaise (optional)

Method

Combine ingredients and refrigerate before serving.

Little packets containing dehydrated buttermilk and seasonings convert sour cream into ranch-flavored dip in the same manner as that of Lipton's now classic dip.

Other forms of sour cream include *crema* (Mexico and Central America), *mileram* or *pavlaka* (Balkans), *schmand* (Germany), *smântână* (Romania), *smetana* (Belarus, Bulgaria, Czech Republic, Finland, Slovenia, Russia, and Ukraine), *smietana* (Poland), *smotana* (Slovakia), *tejföl* (Hungary), and *vrhnje* (Croatia).[2] The *kaymak* of Afghanistan, Central Asia, Greece, India, Iran, Iraq, Turkey, and parts of the Balkans is slightly firmer and less tart than sour cream. It is made from cow, goat, sheep, or water buffalo milk that has been reduced by long cooking before being lightly fermented. In the Balkans, beef simmers in *kaymak*, or a dollop of it melts atop patties of ground meat.

Unlike the dairy products just described, the clotted cream of the British Isles is not fermented at all. It is heated and skimmed until a buttery layer (64 percent fat on average) forms that can be skimmed off the top. In the heating process, numerous new compounds are formed (mostly from the breakdown of lactose), giving the cream a complex, almost nutlike sweetness. It is generally used in desserts or to add a luxurious touch to a "cream tea," when it's spread on scones along with strawberry preserves. It can also add richness when stirred into risotto or even mashed potatoes just before service. Indian *malai*, which has 55 percent butterfat, is made from buffalo milk the same way as clotted cream, by heating and skimming, but is used in a wide variety of sweet and savory dishes, notably the sweet liquid by which balls of *paneer* (a fresh cheese) become dessert.

Yogurt is made everywhere that dairy products are consumed. The milk (of cows or whatever dairy animals one has—perhaps literally—at hand: camels, goats, horses, sheep, water buffalos, even yaks) is first heated, then inoculated with a culture of *Lactobacillus delbrueckii* subsp. *Bulgaricus* or *Streptococcus thermophilus*. It's an ancient substance; Galen wrote, at the end of the second century, in his book on the properties of foodstuffs that even those with sensitive stomachs "tolerate oxygala without harm when it has been surrounded with snow."[3] The yogurt may then be strained to rid it of excess moisture. In the United States, that strained (well-drained) yogurt is marketed as "Greek yogurt," though actual Greek yogurt is much firmer, practically cheese. Some strained yogurts are additionally thickened with butterfat or dehydrated milk powder.

Yogurt is sold—strained or not—in full-fat, low-fat, and nonfat versions. The reduced fat varieties are artificially thickened with guar gum, locust bean gum, pectin, and/or various starches (modified or not). If the yogurt is intended to thicken a cooked sauce, it is important to use the full-fat type; low- and nonfat versions will curdle at high temperatures. Even full-fat yogurts can curdle if overheated. They are best added at the very end of cooking (though some Indian cooks add a starch, such as chickpea flour, to help prevent curdling). Flavored yogurts, in countless variations, attempt to ameliorate yogurt's natural lactic tang. In cooking one should use only plain yogurt, whether strained or not.

Many dipping sauces capitalize on yogurt's tartness. Greek *tzatziki* is somewhere between a salad and a sauce—chopped cucumber and herbs (parsley and/or mint and/or dill) swim in yogurt redolent of garlic and lemon juice, well seasoned with olive oil, pepper, and salt. The yogurt is typically fermented milk from goats or sheep. Iraqi *jajeek* is virtually identical. Turkish *cacik* is similar but may also include dill, thyme, and sour sumac. If cucumbers are replaced by carrots and/or lettuce, *cacik* becomes *havuç tarator*. If strained yogurt (*labneh*) is used and vegetables are omitted, *cacik* becomes *haydari*. Syrian *labneh* is well-drained yogurt, left to age a bit to become tarter, then mixed with olive oil and mint. In Iran, a *cacik*-like dish adds chopped nuts and raisins; it's called *mâst-o-khiâr*. *Mâst-chekide* is yogurt mixed with a watered-down purée of mixed herbs—basil, cilantro, and parsley—while *mâst-musir* is yogurt combined with wild shallots. Throughout the Balkans, strained yogurt is combined with cucumbers, garlic, and chopped walnuts to make *tarator*. An Iraqi sauce of cooked yogurt (*laban*), thickened with corn starch and perfumed with mint, is served with *kubba*—fried meat-filled dumplings. *Raita* is like the *tzatziki* of the Asian subcontinent: it's yogurt, cucumber, mint, and sometimes cilantro and toasted cumin seeds. Occasionally minced chile peppers are added, though *raitas* are generally meant to cool the palate following very spicy dishes. Dozens of variations on *raita* exist, mostly as side dishes, with vegetables, fruits, and even *dals* (pulses) stirred into the seasoned yogurt.

Yogurt is, in a sense, the mother sauce of all these dip-like sauces.

Quark is made by gently warming, then straining soured milk. Its fermentation is carried out by mesophilic *Lactococcus* bacteria (which thrive at lower temperatures than the thermophilic species used in making yogurt). It is like a firm Greek yogurt, bordering on soft cheese. *Skyr* is a Scandinavian product, similar to *quark* (though it's less thoroughly cooked and may use rennet to coagulate the raw milk). It's primarily consumed in Iceland, where it originated in the days of that nation's literary sagas, but is now—along with similar products—popular in the United Kingdom, Germany, the Baltic states, and as far south as Italy, as far east as the Balkans, and as far west as Canada. An Icelandic dipping sauce, *skyronnes*, is made by thinning *skyr* with olive oil to the consistency of mayonnaise or sour cream and flavoring it with garlic and herbs—typically basil. It's served with fish and chips, a variation on aioli, which is more interesting than American tartar sauce or the malt vinegar served in the United Kingdom.

We've seen that milk and cream are oil-in-water emulsions (while butter is a water-in-oil emulsion), but cheeses operate a little differently. Depending on its water content (which varies according to how it is produced and its age), a cheese may or may not melt well. In fondues, Welsh rabbit, and some *queso* recipes, additional liquid (such as wine or beer) can make nonmelting cheese more amenable to becoming fluid again. Some of the most flavorful cheeses, like Gruyère and Parmigiano-Reggiano, don't have sufficient water to melt normally. Almost all fondues employ a small amount of wine to aid in the melting process. However, adding sodium citrate to a liquid component, then introducing the hard cheese a bit at a time (just as one adds oil to water in forming other emulsions) produces the desired unctuous texture. The prototypical never-curdling cheese product, Velveeta, uses sodium citrate for this purpose—as well as sodium alginate (an emulsifying thickener made from seaweed), a number of milk-derived ingredients, and cheese culture. It cannot legally describe itself as "cheese"; it's a "pasteurized prepared cheese product." Cheez Whiz, like Velveeta, is a mélange of chemicals—citric acid, emulsifiers, and stabilizers (carrageenan and xanthan gum)—artificially colored with annatto. Like Velveeta, it actually contains cheese, albeit in some unusual forms; one version is packaged in an aerosol can, allowing it to be sprayed onto foods. Fast-food nachos are sometimes slathered with Cheez Whiz as a rough surrogate for *queso con chile*, a Mexican dipping sauce roughly analogous to fondue.

This concludes the technical portion of this examination of sauces, their properties, and their preparation. It is not, however, the end of our explorations. We've seen hints so far of the next chapter's subject—because it's inescapable. The next chapter is a curious recapitulation of Auguste Escoffier's idea for creating a generation of new sauces by building on existing sauces. For lack of a better term, let's just call them "composites."

12

COMPOSITES

Under Auguste Escoffier's system, the five mother sauces could be used to produce countless daughter sauces, just by adding more ingredients. For example, *sauce béchamel* becomes *sauce mornay* when Gruyère cheese is melted into it (and further enriched with egg yolk). American mac and cheese is a variation in which cooked macaroni are bound with a béchamel containing yellow cheddar cheese, then baked. British cheddar sauce is similar—cheddar cheese melted in béchamel but flavored with prepared mustard and Worcestershire sauce. If onions are slowly cooked in butter, puréed, added to béchamel, and then enriched with heavy cream, the mixture becomes *sauce soubise*. Here's Escoffier's version (note that he includes, in parentheses, the number for a subrecipe to be employed):

Historic Recipe: Sauce Soubise

Cook in butter two lbs. of finely minced onions, scalded for three minutes and well dried. This cooking of the onions in butter increases their flavor. Now add one-half pint of thickened Béchamel (28); season with salt and a teaspoon of powdered sugar. Cook gently for half an hour, rub through a fine sieve, and complete the sauce with some tablespoons of cream and two oz. of butter.[1]

The same basic béchamel assumes a different color and becomes *sauce américaine* with the addition of tomato purée (and a tiny amount of cayenne).[2]

Another pink crustacean-enhanced béchamel, *sauce Nantua*, gets its color and flavor from the addition of crayfish tails and butter enriched with cream.

Hollandaise becomes *sauce maltaise* with the addition of blood orange or sour orange juice. To make *sauce béarnaise*, begin a hollandaise with some chervil, lemon juice, shallots, tarragon, vinegar, white wine, black pepper, and cayenne (or Tabasco) that have been simmered together, strained, and reduced until practically dry (*au sec*) before emulsifying clarified butter in the fragrant residue. Substitute mint for béarnaise's tarragon, and you've got *sauce paloise*. *Sauce béarnaise* in turn becomes *sauce choron* by adding tomato paste. *Sauce valois* is béarnaise plus demi-glace. Add white wine to *valois*, and it becomes *sauce Colbert*.[3]

Ordinary velouté—in this case, a roux-thickened sauce of fish stock—becomes white wine sauce with the addition of heavy cream, lemon juice, and (obviously) wine. Turn it into *sauce Bercy* by sharpening its acidity with lemon juice and white wine in the same way, but flavoring it with shallots, enriching with butter instead of cream, and garnishing with chopped parsley. Cream, egg yolks, and the liquid expressed by cooking mushrooms and oysters transforms fish-based velouté into *sauce normande*. Velouté flavored with celery, leeks, onions, and mushrooms becomes a lighter version of *sauce soubise* (that is, based not on velouté but on béchamel); it's called *sauce bretonne*.

Velouté made with veal stock becomes *sauce allemande* by adding heavy cream, lemon juice, and egg yolks. Chicken-based velouté becomes *sauce poulette* by adding lemon juice, mushrooms, and parsley or the richer *sauce suprême aux champignons* by adding crème fraîche and mushrooms, thickened with *beurre manié*. In this next version, Mrs. W. G. Waters simplified the production of *sauce suprême* not merely by anglicizing it but also by substituting béchamel and stock for velouté.

Historic Recipe: Supreme Sauce

Ingredients

White sauce, fowl stock, butter [cream]

Method

Put three-quarters of a pint of white sauce into a saucepan, and when it is nearly boiling add half a cup of concentrated fowl stock. Reduce until the sauce is quite thick, and when about to serve pass it through a tamis into a bain-marie and add two tablespoonsful of cream.[4]

Sauce espagnole, Escoffier's basic brown sauce, can become *sauce Robert* with a little tweaking—and a lot of evaporation (the "half-glaze" mentioned is sauce *espagnole*, reduced by half, also known as demi-glace).

Historic Recipe: Sauce Robert

Finely mince a large onion and put it into a saucepan with butter. Fry the onion gently and without letting it brown. Dilute with one-third pint of white wine, reduce the latter by one-third, add one pint of half-glaze (23), and leave to simmer for twenty minutes. When serving, finish the sauce with one tablespoon of meat glaze (15), one teaspoon of dry mustard, and one pinch of powdered sugar. If, when finished, the sauce has to wait, it should be kept warm in a double boiler, as it must not boil again.[5]

An even simpler adaptation of *sauce espagnole* is meant to cut through the fatty richness of pork. Simply stir finely chopped cornichons into the classic brown sauce and voilà: *sauce charcutière*! A more familiar dish—in which sharply flavored sauce contrasts with fat flesh—is *canard à l'orange*. Its sauce, based on *espagnole* with tangy citrus juice, has been around at least since the days of Antoine Carême. This recipe is from one of Carême's students, Charles Elmé Francatelli:

Historic Recipe: Bigarrade Sauce

With the carcasses of two or more roasted ducks, make an essence; clarify it, and reduce it to half glaze. To this add a small *ragout*-spoonful of worked *espagnole*, the juice of one orange, and the rind of two others entirely free from any portion of the white pith; and having cut the rind into diamond shapes, blanch these pieces for three minutes in boiling water, and then put them into the sauce, which, after boiling for five minutes, pour into a *bain-marie* for use.[6]

Sauce chasseur, or hunter's sauce, adds mushrooms and shallots to *sauce espagnole*. Many dishes that incorporate mushrooms—bearing names like *cacciatore* and *jaeger*—suggest that sometimes hunters returned from afield not with game but with the fungi that appear in autumn's fields and forests.

Espagnole morphs into *sauce africaine* when basil, bay leaf, garlic, parsley, white wine, and thyme are added—along with vegetables: bell peppers, onions, and tomatoes. Why exactly it's called *africaine* is one of many Gallic mysteries. Perhaps the "Africans" to which it refers were from Louisiana, as that combination of seasonings is more New World Cajun than Old World African.

So, Escoffier's system merely takes a few basic sauces and alters them with different flavorings and/or garnishes to create additional, subsidiary sauces. It's a very effective system—as long as one begins with Escoffier's classic French sauces. However, our kitchens are nothing like Escoffier's hotel restaurant kitchens, and our gastronomic practices do not conform to his notions of proper sauces. Cooks around the world, many of whom have never even heard of Escoffier, have independently stumbled upon the efficient use of preexisting sauces to build new ones. As Harold McGee wrote, "The sauces that cooks actually make are seldom simple suspensions, molecular dispersions, emulsions, or foams. They are usually a combination of two or more."[7]

You may have noticed that many of the sauce categories we've discussed so far were already composites in that they began with solutions (such as stock, vinegar, or wine) and built from there. A simple example is ketchup; it consists of minute particles of tomato pulp suspended in a solution of vinegar, salt, sugar, and infused spices. The composite variations here are more complexly layered. For instance, an emulsion, gel, or cultured protein (or any combination of them), based originally on some form of solution, might be combined with one or more others or garnished with one or more suspended ingredients.

Clear beef bouillon and vinegar, if thickened with an emulsion of cream and egg yolks, spiced with a bit of prepared mustard (itself a suspension in a solution), and garnished with grated horseradish (creating another suspension), yield Albert sauce—a classic British accompaniment for braised beef.

As we've seen, butter is a natural emulsion (an unusual one in which the aqueous phase is suspended in the lipid phase). It can easily become a composite sauce merely by adding other ingredients. These so-called compound butters can be grouped into savory and sweet types. Among the former, *beurre à la bourguignonne* (garlic and parsley butter) is a sauce we associate so much with escargot that it's often called "snail butter." That same butter, minus the parsley, is the sauce for scampi. *Beurre maitre d'hotel* is made by massaging parsley and lemon juice into slightly softened butter. It is then formed into a cylinder and chilled to firm it and allow the flavors to merge. A small slice of the cold compound butter is placed atop hot food (such as a steak) just at service, where it melts before the diner's eyes, forming a sauce. A variation swaps cilantro and lime for parsley and lemon to yield a quick and elegant topping for grilled fish. Café de Paris butter is a variation on *beurre maitre d'hotel*. It omits lemon juice but, in addition to parsley, includes a host of other flavorings—herbs (chives, dill, marjoram, rosemary, tarragon), spices (curry powder, paprika), and aromatics (garlic, shallots)— and receives a blast of umami from anchovies and Worcestershire sauce. A cold slice is served, just as with *beurre maitre d'hotel*, ready to melt into an instant, unctuous sauce. *Sauce chateaubriand*, a classic accompaniment to steak, is made by simmering bay leaves, mushrooms, shallots, thyme, and tarragon in white wine and brown veal stock until they're reduced, straining the resulting liquid, and mounting with *beurre maitre d'hotel* (as in classic *beurre blanc* sauce) just before service.

A sweet compound butter can be prepared by beating honey or maple syrup into softened butter, then forming and chilling it, as with the savory versions. Honey butter makes an interesting sauce for fried chicken (whether with waffles or biscuits). Maple compound butter can be tweaked with some combination of bourbon, cinnamon, citrus zest, or minced dried cranberries—and might add holiday flavor to waffles, sweet potatoes, or biscuits and dinner rolls.

Cocktail sauces accompany shellfish, like cold cooked shrimp, fried calamari or clams, or raw or deep-fried oysters. The American version is simply ketchup mixed with horseradish and sometimes Tabasco. In Great Britain and Western Europe, "cocktail sauce" is not primarily ketchup, as it is in the United States. It begins with a base of mayonnaise but develops a pink color with a small amount of tomato sauce. It's more akin to Russian dressing (which is a little more complex than just mayonnaise and ketchup; it's enhanced by chives, horseradish, pimentos, and spices). In Mississippi, a local version—"comeback sauce"—serves as a dip for fried foods, in addition to its usual job as a salad dressing (especially in coleslaw). The Costa Rican version is *ensalada derepollo*.

Another British cocktail sauce, Marie Rose, was invented during the 1960s but peaked in popularity in the following decade. It began with mayonnaise and a tomato product (purée or paste)—like so many others—but departed from them by adding lemon juice, black pepper, Worcestershire sauce, and sometimes cayenne or Tabasco.[8]

Belgians' famous *pommes frites* are frequently dipped in a similar pink mayonnaise concoction. *Sauce andalouse*—oddly enough—has nothing whatsoever to do with any part of Spain (unless, as some hypothesize, mayonnaise originated in Spain). It is, however, a mixture of tomato paste and mayonnaise, garnished with bits of roasted red pepper. That is the way Escoffier prepared it, except his red peppers were julienned, not chopped. Raymond Sokolov went in another direction altogether, making a lighter, less viscous sauce.

Historic Recipe: Sauce Andalouse

Ingredients

1 cup	ordinary velouté
2 Tbsp.	tomato paste
1 clove	garlic, crushed
2 Tbsp.	red bell pepper, peeled, seeded, and diced
1 Tbsp.	butter
1½ tsp.	parsley, chopped

Method

1. Reduce velouté to ¾ cup in non-reactive pan.
2. Sauté pepper in butter until softened.
3. Whisk in the tomato paste, garlic, and the diced and sautéed pepper. Hold in a bain-marie until ready to serve. At the last minute sprinkle with parsley.[9]

In the 1920s, an Argentinian chemist developed his own version of Russian dressing. His sauce is garnished with roasted red peppers, à la Escoffier, plus cumin and oregano. He called his invention *salsa golf*. Luis Federico Leloir eventually won the Nobel Prize . . . but not for his sauce (the award instead had something to do with the metabolic properties of sugar nucleotides). Columbian *salsa rosado* is much the same thing as *salsa golf*, while Puerto Rican *mayokétchup* makes no attempt to hide the sauce's origins.

In the spring of 2018, the Heinz company floated the idea of a new condiment, called "mayochup," which created something of a storm. The immediate backlash came from many directions, but they all focused on the fact that everyone already knew the mixture by other names. "Some on Twitter even accused Heinz of 'appropriating,' 'gentrifying' or even 'colonizing' the beloved mayo-ketchup combination."[10]

In Utah, the mixture of mayonnaise and ketchup is simply known as "fry sauce"—because it's intended as a dip for French fries. It is seasoned with salt and some undisclosed spices (have you ever seen a commercial sauce or condiment that didn't boast about its "secret spices"?). Texans, who have never been accused of permitting the bland to lead the bland, add hot sauce to the mixture and call it "Raising Cane."

Basic Russian dressing is the so-called special sauce served on "billions and billions" of hamburgers every year.[11] Oddly enough, Russian dressing has even found its way to Russia, the one place where it was *not* invented. Conveniently, it's known there as *ketchunez* (literally, "ketchup-mayonnaise" and pronounced "ketch-onnaise"). The Russian love of mayonnaise is so well known that Turks used to call the emulsion "Russian salad." However, Turkey is a NATO member, so that changed in the 1960s. Cold War politics caused Turks to rename the sauce "American salad."

American tartar sauce is one of a number of other mayonnaise-based sauces. It's garnished with finely chopped pickles or pickle relish. Tartar sauce is a much simplified version of French rémoulade: aioli or mayonnaise, in its most classic form, with added capers, minced cornichon pickles and shallots, mustard, and vinegar, garnished with fresh herbs (chervil, chives, *salad burnet*, and/or tarragon). The main difference between tartar and rémoulade is tartar's lack of anchovy. As might be expected, the Cajun version of mayonnaise-based rémoulade is spicier and more colorful than most others, including that of Louisiana's other cuisine, Creole. It can be studded with bits of celery and parsley, but the main difference is the presence of black pepper, cayenne, mustard, and (in a nod to another familiar mayonnaise competitor) ketchup. Rarely shy with seasonings, Cajun cooks might toss in capers, chopped pickles, horseradish, hot sauce, Worcestershire, raw garlic, and a splash of vinegar to brighten things up.

Thousand Island dressing is a thinned-down version of rémoulade often amended with a wide assortment of flavoring ingredients. It's usually more complex than Utah's fry sauce (or that so-called secret sauce on a certain hamburger chain's products). As with Russian dressing, mayonnaise and ketchup are the primary components, but variations might contain one or more of the following ingredients or garnishes, finely minced: bell peppers or pimentos, chestnuts, chili sauce, chives, cream, garlic, hard-boiled egg, onions, mustard, green olives, orange juice, paprika, parsley, pickles, Tabasco, tomato purée, vinegar, walnuts, or Worcestershire sauce.

Green Goddess dressing was invented in a hotel kitchen in the 1920s and named for a popular movie of the day. It is part of a long history of green sauces, most of which are emulsions combined with suspended ingredients, primarily fresh herbs, which provide the green coloring. It is based on mayonnaise plus some sour cream, flavored with anchovy paste and lemon juice plus herbs—chervil, chives, parsley, and tarragon—and marketed in bottled form, though it has fallen somewhat out of fashion.[12] Attempts to revive it often involve more modern garnishes and placement of the sauce beneath the salad, where it doesn't appear heavy or gloppy.

Recipe: Some Quick Mayonnaise Hacks

These can be made using homemade or prepared mayonnaise.

1. Mix mayonnaise with minced garlic as a substitute for aioli.
2. Stir madras curry powder into mayonnaise for a spicy sandwich spread or salad dressing.
3. Add minced garlic, Worcestershire sauce, anchovy paste, and lemon juice to mayonnaise for an easy Caesar salad dressing (and one that quells any health fears one might have about consuming raw egg yolks).
4. Spread mayonnaise mixed with grated Parmigiano-Reggiano, minced garlic, and parsley before toasting slices of French bread.
5. Spread mayonnaise, minced garlic, and tomato *concassée* on slices of baguette, then bake until bubbly and lightly browned.

Anchoïade provençale is a much more intense mayonnaise-based sauce. The first thing you'll notice when it is served is the distinct aroma of the anchovies pounded into tiny fragments and suspended throughout the sauce. There may also be olives and herbs, which only intensify its deep umami character.

Ketchup and mayonnaise are no longer ingredients in the arsenal of Western sauciers alone.

The Japanese incorporate ketchup in their *tonkatsu* dipping sauce (often served with strips of crisp-fried breaded pork). They combine it with another Western sauce, Worcestershire,[13] or soy sauce, plus garlic, ginger, mirin, or sake (if sake is used, salt and sugar are needed). The Japanese have also taken to mayonnaise, but theirs incorporates mirin, MSG, and hot sauce—often *sriracha*.

Dipping sauces in the Philippines are often made by mixing other sauces (or proto-sauces), such as fish sauce, honey, soy, or vinegar, and then suspending garnishes of aromatics, herbs, and spices. This is a typically sour example:

Recipe: Filipino Sour Dipping Sauce

Ingredients

2 Tbsp.	tamarind paste
2 cloves	garlic, thinly sliced
1 tsp.	fresh ginger, coarsely grated
1 Tbsp.	honey
1 tsp.	sugar
1 Tbsp.	soy sauce
2 tsp.	fish sauce (such as *patís*)
½ tsp.	crushed chile flakes
to taste	salt and pepper

Method

1. Soften the tamarind paste with a little water and strain to eliminate any hard seeds.
2. Grind all ingredients in mortar and pestle, or food processor, until smooth.[14]

In Guam, dipping sauces called *fina'denne* are ubiquitous. They're made in two basic forms: a dark "black" version based on soy sauce and tuba vinegar (fermented from the sap of coconut palms) and a light "white" version made with either vinegar or citrus juices and fishy brine. *Fina'denne* is often customized with some combination of salt, onion, garlic, hot chile, and/or tomato.

Michel Guérard's *sauce vierge* would normally be classed as a form of vinaigrette (since it's made of olive oil and lemon juice). However, it also contains suspended bits of minced basil and tomato (and various other herbs and spices, as the dish requires) that flavor the sauce by infusion if heated or maceration if not.

Caruso sauce is a Uruguayan cross between cheese/cream Alfredo and béchamel (but adding beef broth to the milk), garnished with smoked ham, sautéed mushrooms and onions, and nuts. A simpler version is actually just béchamel flavored with nutmeg and cinnamon and studded with toasted walnuts and ham (but no cheese). Still another Caruso sauce is a tomato purée enriched with chicken livers. It has no connection to the Uruguayan specialty.

In another decadently rich composite sauce from across the Atlantic, cooked chicken livers seasoned with thyme blossoms are finely ground and suspended in a mixture of reduced heavy cream and Dijon mustard. Just before service, butter is stirred in to form Café de Paris sauce.[15] It either tops or is topped by an *entrecôte* (steak). It's not a dish for the cholesterol-averse.

Puerto Rico provides a number of examples of noncommercial hot sauces that are part suspension, part emulsion. The liquid phase of *ajilimójili's* cooked emulsion can be any combination of various citrus juices and various vinegars, while the lipid phase is usually olive oil. The flavorings suspended in the emulsion are bits of minced chiles (habaneros, Scotch bonnets, and/ or gentleman's peppers—*Capsicum frutescens 'Ají caballero'*), plus cilantro or *culantro* (*Eryngium foetidum*).

A sweeter version uses *ají dulce* (which is the same species as the fiery habanero—*Capsicum chinense*—but a variety that lacks habanero's heat) in place of the hot peppers and adds butter, honey, and tomatoes. A green version, *pique verde boricua*, is the same as *ajilimójili* but substitutes *cubanelles* (Italian frying peppers, *Capsicum annuum*) and gentleman's peppers for the hot chiles. *Mojito isleño* is generally served with seafood. To make it, garlic, onions, and bell peppers are first cooked in olive oil; then bay leaf, chopped capers, olives, and tomatoes, vinegar, salt, and pepper are added and cooked until soft.

Chinese barbecue sauce (*char siu* or *siu haau*) shares only a few characteristics with the American barbecue sauces—especially Kansas City–style sauces. Both deliver the requisite sweet, spicy, and sour components (in *siu haau*, from garlic, honey, palm sugar, five spice powder, and pepper), but from there they head in different directions. The Chinese sauce adds a lot of umami via soy sauce, oyster sauce, and hoisin sauce (see chapter 9, "Gels").

A much more complex variation on Chinese barbecue sauce (*sha cha jiang*) increases the umami almost exponentially by incorporating dried

Three of the primary ingredients in many Chinese sauces: soy, sesame oil, and ginger. Garlic and scallions would complete many of them. *Source:* Gary Allen

seafood—oysters, scallops, and shrimp—in a solution prepared from shrimp heads and shells with rice vinegar and soy sauce. The sauce also contains suspended particles of lemon zest, peanuts, and *doubanjiang* (a bottled paste of chiles, garlic, and fermented soybeans).

Most Chinese American places (especially those that specialize in take-out) serve a similar brown sauce because most such establishments make it in bulk from a common list of ingredients—many of which are already sauces in their own right. As in Escoffier's restaurant-based system, this is a mother sauce that can be tweaked for use with different dishes. If you examine this list of ingredients, you'll note that many of them serve to boost the umami of the final product.

Recipe: Basic Chinese Restaurant Brown Sauce

Ingredients

12 oz.	rich chicken stock, unsalted
8½ Tbsp.	Kikkoman soy sauce
5 Tbsp.	Amoy Gold Label soy sauce
1 Tbsp.	mushroom-flavored dark soy sauce
2 Tbsp.	hoisin sauce
5 Tbsp.	oyster sauce
5 Tbsp.	sugar
3 Tbsp.	MSG
6 Tbsp.	white wine (such as pinot grigio)
4 Tbsp.	Shaoxing rice wine
1 Tbsp.	sesame oil
3 slices	fresh ginger, minced
2 cloves	garlic, minced
1	scallion, white parts only, chopped
to taste	white pepper (plus salt if needed)

Method

1. Combine all ingredients but the last and simmer until fragrant.
2. Taste for seasoning and add salt and pepper if needed.
3. Sauce can be modified with extra garlic, or ginger, or black vinegar and sugar, or hot chile paste to serve in different dishes.[16]

Pan sauces are exactly what their name suggests: they are made in the pan used for cooking the main course (as opposed to being made in a separate sauce pan) and acquire some of their flavor from the primary ingredients. Most gravies and classic sauces—like the *beurre blanc* and *beurre rouge* we've already discussed—are pan sauces.

Shrewsbury sauce is a kind of pan sauce usually made with roast lamb. After the meat is done, most of the fat is poured off, and the pan is deglazed with port, some red currant jelly, a bit of mustard, and a splash of lemon juice and/or Worcestershire sauce. Flour is added to thicken (adjusting the viscosity with stock, as needed). Cumberland sauce is also based on red currant jelly, port, and mustard but has a zippier flavor because it adds ginger and pepper, plus citrusy notes from the zest of bitter Seville oranges. It is not thickened with flour but merely reduced somewhat.

South Africans have a different—and sometimes more tongue-in-cheek—approach to saucing their meats. They splash monkey gland sauce on everything from chicken to burgers to spare ribs to steak. The sauce has a lot of ingredients, many of them prepared sauces. The following recipe is a relatively simple one (others might include chutney, mustard, soy sauce, and/or wine). None involve actual monkey parts—glandular or otherwise.

Recipe: Monkey Gland Sauce

Ingredients

1 tsp.	olive oil
1	small onion, very finely chopped
1 clove	garlic
1	large tomato, peeled, seeded, and finely chopped
1 Tbsp.	white wine vinegar
1 Tbsp.	cold water
1 tsp.	black pepper, coarsely ground
1 Tbsp.	sun-dried tomato paste
1 Tbsp.	Worcestershire sauce
1 Tbsp.	dark brown sugar
1 tsp.	Tabasco sauce

Method

Gently sauté the onions and garlic until soft and golden, then add all the other sauce ingredients and simmer briskly for 3 minutes, stirring occasionally. Reserve the sauce on low heat [and spoon the hot sauce over meat].[17]

Commercial condiments can in themselves be combinations of other sauces. The next two are nineteenth-century versions of knockoff, home-made takes on commercial products (much like those found on countless websites today). Both call for "mushroom catchup," which was not as viscous as tomato ketchup. Eliza Leslie published this composite sauce in 1853:

Historic Recipe: Harvey's Sauce

Dissolve six anchovies in a pint of strong vinegar, and then add to them three table-spoonfuls of India soy, and three table-spoonfuls of mushroom catchup, two heads of garlic bruised small, and a quarter of an ounce of cayenne. Add sufficient cochineal powder to colour the mixture red. Let all these ingredients infuse in the vinegar for a fortnight, shaking it every day, and then strain and bottle it for use. Let the bottles be small, and cover the corks with leather.[18]

She also included this similar sauce:

Historic Recipe: Quin's Sauce

Pound in a mortar six large anchovies, moistening them with their own pickle.
Then chop and pound six small onions.

Mix them with a little black pepper and a little cayenne, half a glass of soy, four glasses of mushroom catchup, two glasses of claret, and two of black walnut pickle.

Put the mixture into a small sauce-pan or earthen pipkin, and let it simmer slowly till all the bones of the anchovies are dissolved.

Strain it, and when cold, bottle it for use; dipping the cork in melted rosin, and tying leather over it. Fill the bottles quite full.[19]

Another nineteenth-century British condiment, Wow-Wow sauce, was built on a foundation of mushroom ketchup. It added prepared mustard, pickled cucumbers and walnuts, port, and vinegar. It boosted its umami quotient with beef stock, then thickened it with butter and flour (it's not clear whether these last ingredients were in the form of roux or *beurre manié*, though roux seems more likely).

Basic sauces, like ketchup and Worcestershire, are often combined to make new condiments, and some of them are indigenous to very specific locations.

While horseradish is merely a suspension of grated root in vinegar (and sometimes beet juice), horseradish sauce is a composite of grated root with an emulsion (such as mayonnaise) or a starch-thickened gel (like salad dressing or one of the forms of cream sauce that doesn't include actual cream), plus flavorings like garlic, onion, salt, and sugar.

Almost all barbecue sauces build on combinations of prepared sauces that might be solutions, suspensions, or emulsions (ketchup, mustard, and Worcestershire are typical); indeed, Australian "barbecue sauce" is often nothing but ketchup and Worcestershire. By the way, "tomato sauce" is Australian for ketchup.

Barbecue (which, as any aficionado will argue, is not the same as back-yard grilling) originated in the Caribbean and takes its name from the grill of sticks that held the meat, called a *barbecoa*. Barbecue sauce began as a basting liquid to keep the long- and slow-cooked meats from drying out. Basting the meat with flavorful sauce is still the preferred method, though in the Caribbean it's called jerking. Jerk sauce shares barbecue sauce's complex sweet-sour-spicy nature but has a distinctly tropical twist. Typical ingredients include fresh thyme (possibly the region's local wild herb, Cuban oregano, *Plectratbhus amboinicus*, which is strongly redolent of thyme's principal flavoring compound, thymol), allspice, black pepper, cinnamon, dark brown sugar, garlic, fresh ginger, nutmeg, lime juice, scallions, Scotch bonnet peppers, and—as we'll see with many barbecue sauces—a couple of prepared sauces: soy sauce and ketchup.

However, there is a truly American urge to "improve" on anything that is already good—often by adding whatever is on hand. That usually means other condiments. Consequently, a widely differing range of barbecue sauce styles has evolved based upon local preferences and/or ingredients. One commercial line of barbecue sauces, which pretends to be from Tennessee, is flavored with Jack Daniels whiskey. It's actually made by a huge corporation headquartered in Pittsburgh, Pennsylvania.

The recipes for barbecue sauces vary greatly and are strongly regional. For example, there is a sharp dividing line between the barbecue sauces of eastern and western North Carolina. In the east, the sauce is based on vinegar, brown sugar, cayenne, Tabasco (or similar pepper sauce), and black pepper. In the west, pit masters add butter, ketchup, lemon juice, mustard, and Worcestershire. In South Carolina, a very different kind of barbecue sauce reigns supreme. Since many German immigrants settled the area, mustard is foremost in the mix—while western North Carolina's sauce features some mustard, South Carolina's barbecue sauces are positively yellow from it.

Memphis barbecue sauces are thin, like those of the Carolinas, but they are sweetened with tomato. On the other side of the Appalachians, barbecue sauces get thicker (containing reduced tomato sauce) and, very often, sweeter. Kansas City's style—like that of the famous Arthur Bryant—is a deep russet color, sweet and tangy. When most people (outside the areas already mentioned) think of "barbecue sauce," this is what comes to mind—in part because large-scale commercial BBQ sauces, such as those produced by Heinz (which includes several under the Jack Daniels brand name) and KC Masterpiece, began with Kansas City–style recipes. These companies also produce marinades and steak sauces.

As one moves south, molasses darkens the sauce even more. Moving west, the sauce takes on Tex-Mex overtones, incorporating chili powder and cumin and the smoky mesquite-flavored drippings from a beef brisket. In this, Texas departs from almost all other barbecue styles (pork and chicken are the proteins of choice in most regions).

Barbecue sauces come in even more specific—that is, more narrowly geographically defined—variations. For example, in parts of Alabama, you might encounter the strangest barbecue sauce in the United States. This sauce is not red, brown, or yellow—it is white. A scoop of mayonnaise thinned with cider vinegar and seasoned with a lot of cayenne pepper, celery seeds, garlic, horseradish, mustard, salt, and sugar tops smoky chicken and pork in the northern hill country.

In the region around Louisville, Kentucky, Henry Bain Sauce (originally created at the Pendennis Club, at the very beginning of the twentieth century, specifically to accompany members' wild game) is dominant. Today it is bottled and sold in local grocery stores—and more likely poured on steak or roast beef. It's definitely a composite sauce; it combines chutney (Major Grey's mango-based sauce is classic, though other fruit chutneys are sometimes substituted), ketchup, A.1., Worcestershire, and chili sauce, spiced up with some form of Tabasco-like hot sauce.

Just west of Louisville, a very tart version of barbecue sauce was originally meant to temper the rich gaminess of fatty mutton. The slow-cooked meat is basted continuously with an acidic mixture of cider vinegar, lemon juice, and Worcestershire sauce (well seasoned with salt and pepper). The sauce known as "Owensboro dip" repeats the basting ingredients but adds allspice, brown sugar, garlic powder, and onion salt (plus, if a little more umami is needed, MSG).

The task of cooking true barbecue is long, hot, and smoky—and frequently, but not always, men's work. It's the sort of job that generates a manly (or womanly) thirst, and, as often as not, the thirst quencher of choice is beer. It's almost inconceivable that, at some point or another, some of that

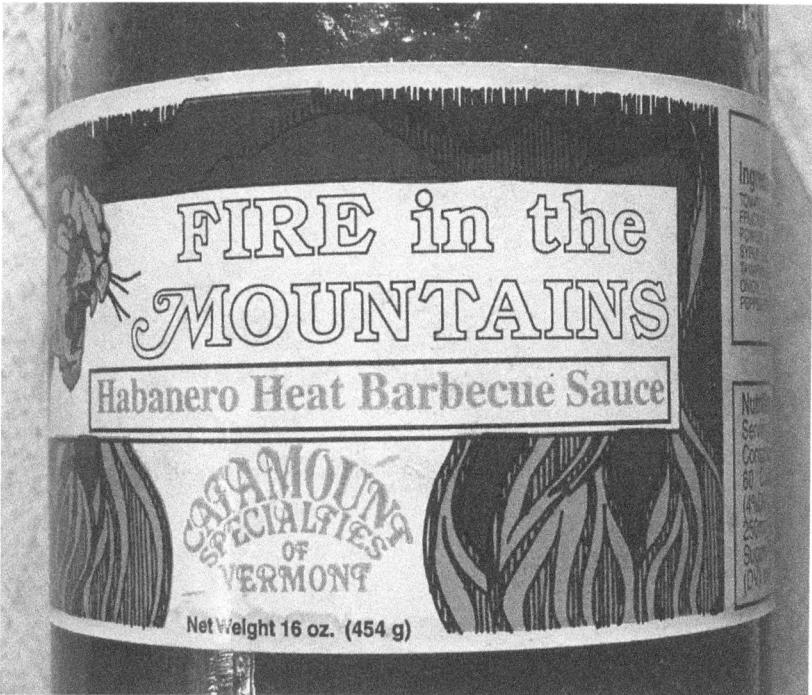

Barbecue, once a primarily Southern phenomenon, is now found everywhere. This one, from New England, features a decidedly non-Yankee ingredient: habaneros. *Source:* Gary Allen

beer would not have found its way into the sauce. A recent Google search for "beer barbecue sauce" garnered more than fifty thousand hits.

Recipes for such BBQ sauces include various beers (which vary from region to region, following the "whatever-is-at-hand" rule), from lite to stout or from fruity lambic to hoppy IPA; hot peppers, from anchos to cayenne, or hot sauces, from Crystal to *sriracha*; and a range of sweeteners from honey or corn syrup to maple syrup to molasses.

Texans love beef brisket for their barbecues, and Jewish cooks love brisket, so we should expect that Jewish cooks who barbecue in the Lone Star State would create their own sauce to serve with unctuously fatty, smoky brisket. The following uncooked BBQ sauce was created in the 1970s using plenty of commercial sauces as ingredients.

Recipe: Austin Jewish Community BBQ Sauce

Ingredients

2 bottles	Heinz ketchup
1 12oz. bottle	Heinz chili sauce
½ bottle	A.1. sauce
dash	Tabasco sauce
1 Tbsp.	soy sauce
⅓ cup	brown mustard
1 can	beer
1 Tbsp.	mustard powder
1½ cups	brown sugar
2 Tbsp.	black pepper
1½ cups	red wine vinegar
1 cup	lemon juice
2 Tbsp.	salad oil
to taste	garlic, minced

Method

Combine all ingredients. Cover and store, refrigerated, until served.[20]

If barbecue cooks are too lazy to make their sauce, several commercial bottled sauces now come in beer variations. For those rare pit masters who don't drink beer, it's possible to thin barbecue sauce recipes with cola, root beer, or Dr Pepper.

In central Africa, the barbecue tradition is strong and reveals a bit of the region's colonial history. The marinade for large cuts of beef, such as brisket or shoulder, is composed of cayenne and umami-rich Maggi sauce[21] from England. The regional term for barbecue, however, is French: *coupé-coupé* (literally, "cut-cut").

Throughout the Great Plains states, Dorothy Lynch Home Style Dressing has been a staple sauce since the 1940s. Based mostly on canned tomato soup (a suspension that has been modified—thickened into a thin gel—with corn starch and rice flour), it's flavored with vinegar and spices and emulsified with soybean oil and xanthan gum. Midwesterners use it as a foundation for dips, barbecue sauces, glazes for meaty appetizers (chicken wings, cocktail wieners, meatballs, sausages, and ribs), and marinades—not to mention variations on the theme of salad dressings. The Dorothy Lynch website even features crowd-sourced recipes for a cake and muffins.

Moving away from barbecue, Sephardic *agristada* is a tangy hollandaise-like sauce that may or may not contain a bit of roux. Egg yolks and lemon juice are first beaten together and then combined with olive oil, plus a small amount of chicken broth or simply warm water. They are cooked together, with more liquid slowly added until the desired consistency is achieved. As the sauce contains no dairy, it can accompany meats (though fried fish and vegetables, especially artichokes, are more frequent plate-mates). If thinned down and garnished with tiny meatballs, the sauce becomes a soup of the same name. *Agristada* is closely related to Greek *avgolemono*, though it was originally soured with verjuice.

Chinese sweet-and-sour sauce—a garishly colored coating for battered and deep-fried chicken, pork, or shrimp in virtually every takeout joint—is a classic example of a composite sauce—"composite" in terms of not only the sauces being combined but also their original provenance. The "sour" comes from vinegar, the salty from soy sauce, the sweet from sugar, the richness and savor from dark, nutty sesame oil, and the almost frightening color from ketchup.[22] This sauce usually envelops the breaded protein (as well as peppers and sometimes pineapple) in gelatinous glory thanks to corn starch.

The original sweet-and-sour pork, from northeastern China, *guo bao rou*, is simpler—and much less garish than that found in Chinese American restaurants. Strips of battered pork are deep-fried, as in the US version, but instead of receiving a thick coating of fluorescent goo, the strips are tossed with a mixture of syrup and vinegar. The potato starch coating lightly thickens the sauce. American sweet-and-sour pork is an adaptation of the Cantonese dish *char siu bao*. Haw Flakes (a kind of candy made from sugar and hawthorn berries), preserved plums, and of course vinegar lend a sweet-tart flavor and reddish coloration. Those qualities are mimicked, unsuccessfully, by ketchup (and sometimes pineapple juice and artificial food coloring) in the United States.

A cooked Vietnamese dipping sauce, *nuốc leo*, begins by frying garlic and bird's eye chiles in oil, adding chopped peanuts, and cooking a bit longer. The liquid components (chicken stock, fish sauce, coconut milk, and hoisin sauce) and a little sugar are added next. The mixture is cooked until it thickens slightly and the oil begins to render out of the peanuts. This combination of solutions and prepared suspensions, plus suspended softened peanuts, is further garnished with chopped toasted peanuts for a bit of crunch.

Another cooked sauce from Vietnam, *sot ca chua*, simmers tomato *concasée* and minced garlic in coconut milk or chicken stock, seasoned with fish sauce and chiles. It's usually poured over fried fish or tofu.

Many Thai dipping sauces (known collectively as *nam chim*) are composites of other sauce types. *Nam chim kai* is the nation's basic sweet chili sauce; it's as omnipresent as ketchup on a Western table. When garnished with chopped peanuts, cilantro, and cucumber, it's called *nam chim thot man* and serves as a dip for fried cakes of crab, fish, or prawns. *Nam chim satay* is made by simmering brown sugar, chiles, lime juice, peanut butter, salt, and shrimp paste in thinned coconut milk. It's the familiar sauce served with skewers of marinated chicken strips. *Achat* or *nam chim taengkwa* is a thin dipping sauce of sweetened vinegar with suspended bits of minced cucumber and hot chile peppers. Another thin sauce, *nam chim thale*, is a sweet-sour-savory blend of fish sauce, lime juice, and dissolved sugar, garnished with minced garlic and chile. Sweet, sticky brown *nam chim chaeo*, served with grilled pork, is made from rice flour that has been toasted until nearly black with chiles, fish sauce, and palm sugar.

Nam chim suki is primarily a sauce used in a hot pot for cooking other foods, but—since it is very pungent—it is also used as a sauce for bland foods, like noodles. It's basically a purée of odoriferous preserved bean curd along with its liquid; prepared chili sauce; fresh bird's eye chiles; garlic, both fresh and pickled (*krathiam dong*), along with juice of the pickled garlic; salt; sugar; malt vinegar; and lime juice. All the ingredients are ground together, thinned with water to the desired consistency, and garnished with sesame seeds and a drizzle of toasted sesame oil.

While most of the sauces discussed in this book are savory, we shouldn't overlook those that are meant for the dessert course. The simplest ones are coulis: sweetened fruit purées, such as raspberry or strawberry, which may or may not be spiked with alcohol. Many dessert sauces are commercial products, and among the most popular are those that feature chocolate as the main ingredient.

Bar chocolate is a solidified suspension of cocoa particles and sugar in cocoa butter. Milk chocolate is the same but with added milk solids. Bar

A quintessential New York sauce used in desserts and to make iconic egg creams. *Source:* Gary Allen

chocolate is also an emulsion of cocoa butter and sugar syrup. One reason we find it so deeply satisfying is that (like another solid emulsion—cold butter) it melts at body temperature. By "melting in one's mouth," a solid morphs into an unctuous fat-rich sauce.

Chocolate syrup is an emulsion of cocoa in corn syrup (stabilized by some mono- and diglycerides and usually some additional xanthan gum). Hot fudge sauce is merely chocolate *ganache* (an emulsion of bar chocolate and heavy cream, sometimes with a bit of butter); it's basically a melted version of a chocolate truffle.

To make caramel sauce, sugar is slowly heated until Maillard reactions turn it golden brown. As that happens, a number of new chemical compounds are created. One of them, diacetyl, in low concentrations, smells and tastes like butter, so butterscotch sauce does not actually need butter for flavor (though it does improve the texture and mouth-feel). Caramel sauce, which would otherwise be a supersaturated solution, generally contains natural emulsions such as milk or heavy cream. Sometimes additional sugar is not even needed—the slow heating of lactose in the milk or cream is sufficient to develop the diacetyl aroma and desired Maillard coloration.

AFTERWORD

The history of sauces is complicated. Some have made concerted efforts to simplify (think Raymond Sokolov's *The Saucier's Apprentice* or Chef André Soltner's reduction of Auguste Escoffier's five mother sauces, *Les Fonds*, to just two stocks: a brown one made from roasted veal bones and mirepoix, and a white one that substitutes unroasted chicken or fish bones for the veal), but they have had only limited—and very narrowly defined—success. In counterpoint to those attempts at simplification, the constant exchange of culinary ideas from other cultures has only added levels of complexity that would never have been imagined by the likes of Taillevant or Antoine Carême.

There are those who believe that sauces are overly fussy, that they merely obscure the flavor of the main ingredient in a dish—or, worse, fraudulently obscure the poor quality of less-than-fresh food. Poppy Cannon once said, "People think French cooking is gooking it up."[1] This is hardly a new idea. For example, in *The Deipnosophistae*, Athenaeus quoted *The Peace*, in which Theopompus complained, somewhat less colloquially, "The weather loaf is nice, but to cheat us with the addition of sauces to the loaves is vicious."[2]

Clearly, anyone who has read all the way to the end of this book is less sauce-averse than was Theopompus. I confess to feeling a tiny frisson of amusement in knowing that this puritan of a Greek historian—who seems not to have known the epicurean pleasures of sauces—is largely forgotten today, while we happily enjoy our saucy version of the good life . . . as long as it's gooked up with the right sauce.

Runny egg yolks: a category of sauce that has not even been considered—"foods that need no other ingredients to provide their own sauce." Perhaps a subject for a later edition? *Source:* Gary Allen

NOTES

A FEW WORDS ABOUT SALT

1. Athenaeus, *The Deipnosophistae*, trans. Charles Burton Gulick (Cambridge, MA: Harvard University Press, 1927–1941), 9:161.

2. Zhou Hongcheng, "Salt and Sauce in the Chinese Culinary," *Flavor & Fortune* 16 (Spring 2009): 9–10.

CHAPTER 1. SO MANY RICH SAUCES

1. Athenaeus, *The Deipnosophistae*, trans. Charles Burton Gulick (Cambridge, MA: Harvard University Press, 1927–1941), 13:414.

2. This comic playwright was a contemporary of Alexander the Great (ca. 323–283 BCE).

3. Athenaeus, *Deipnosophistae*, 3:436.

4. Ibid., 3:58.

5. Ibid., 6:95–97.

6. Ibid., 2:379.

7. The tablets are in Yale University's Babylonian collection. They are more than thirty-seven centuries old.

8. Jean Bottéro, *The Oldest Cuisine in the World: Cooking in Mesopotamia* (Chicago: University of Chicago Press, 2004), 27.

9. Some members of this genus are employed in traditional Chinese medicine to treat erectile dysfunction and urinary tract diseases.

10. Laura Kelley, "New Flavors for the Oldest Recipes," *Aramco World* (November/December 2012).

11. Ibid.

12. Petronius, *The Satyricon*, trans. William Arrowsmith (Ann Arbor: University of Michigan Press, 1959), 33.

13. Juvenal, *The Satires of Juvenal*, trans. Rolfe Humphries (Bloomington: Indiana University Press, 1958), 14:7–9.

14. *Murri* sounds like the Romans' *muria*, and they are related. *Muria* was a lighter sauce; it was the brine in which fish, such as tuna, was preserved. *Liquamen* was a little heavier, being made of tiny fish, such as sardines and anchovies (Vietnamese fish sauce, such as that made by Red Boat, is very similar; it's also made from anchovies). *Garum* was the heaviest, being made from entrails and blood of large fish, like tuna.

15. Zhou, "Salt and Sauce in the Chinese Culinary," 9–10.

16. Ibid.

CHAPTER 2. OLD WINE IN NEW BOTTLES

1. Guillaume Tirel, *Le viandier de Taillevent*, trans. James Prescott, http://www.telusplanet.net/public/prescotj/data/viandier.

2. Ibid.

3. Michel de Montaigne, *The Essays of Michel de Montaigne*, trans. George B. Ives (New York: Heritage Press, 1946), 407.

4. Ibid., 407–8.

5. Anthimus, *Anthimus, De observatione ciborum: On the Observance of Foods*, ed. and trans. Mark Grant (Blackawton, Totnes, Devon, UK: Prospect Books, 1996), 73.

6. Ibid., 79.

7. Joan Santanach, ed., *The Book of Sent Soví: Medieval Recipes from Catalonia*, trans. Robin Vogelzang (Barcelona: Barcino-Tamesis, 2014), 49.

8. Ibid., 83.

9. Samuel Pegge, *The Forme of Cury: A Roll of Ancient English Cookery Compiled, about A.D. 1390*, Project Gutenberg, http://www.gutenberg.org/ebooks/8102.

10. Ibid.

11. Wynkyn de Worde, *The Boke of Keruynge* (East Sussex, UK: Southover Press, 2003), 44.

12. Ibid., 62.

13. T. Sarah Peterson, *Acquired Taste: The French Origins of Modern Cooking* (Ithaca, NY: Cornell University Press 1994), 193–94.

14. Louis, chevalier de Jaucourt, "Sauce," *The Encyclopedia of Diderot & d'Alembert Collaborative Translation Project*, trans. Sean Takats, http://hdl.handle.net/2027/spo.did2222.0000.666.

15. Peterson, *Acquired Taste*, 193.

CHAPTER 3. NINETEENTH CENTURY

1. Ian Kelly, *Cooking for Kings: The Life of Antonin Carême, the First Celebrity Chef* (New York: Walker, 2004), 233.

2. Ibid., 232.

3. Ibid., 234.

4. Ibid., 233–34.

5. Carême was, at various points in his career, employed by Talleyrand, Napoleon, England's King George IV, Russia's Tsar Alexander I, and—in private practice—James Mayer Rothschild.

6. Quoted in Raymond Sokolov, *The Saucier's Apprentice: A Modern Guide to Classic French Sauces for the Home* (New York: Knopf, 1982), 7.

7. Jean Anthelme Brillat-Savarin, *The Physiology of Taste*, trans. M. F. K. Fisher (New York: Limited Editions Club, 1949), 92–93.

8. Ibid., 67.

9. Alexis Benoist Soyer, *The Gastronomic Regenerator: A Simplified and Entirely New System of Cookery, with Nearly Two Thousand Practical Receipts Suited to the Income of All Classes*, 6th ed. (London: Simpkin, Marshall, & Co., Stationers' Hall Court, 1849).

10. "The Original Tomato Sauce," *Vintage Cookbook Trials*, https://vintagecookbooktrials.wordpress.com/2013/04/11/the-original-tomato-sauce.

11. Soyer, *The Gastronomic Regenerator*.

12. Ibid.

13. Ibid.

14. Ibid.

15. Quoted in *Memoirs of Alexis Soyer: With Unpublished Receipts and Odds and Ends of Gastronomy*, ed. F. Volant and J. R. Warren (Cambridge: Cambridge University Press, 2013), 154.

16. Quoted in Ruth Cowen, *Relish: The Extraordinary Life of Alexis Soyer, Victorian Celebrity Chef* (London: Orion Books, 2007), 243.

17. Alexis Soyer, *The Modern Housewife* (New York: D. Appleton & Co., 1851), 65–66.

18. Ibid., 153.

19. Anonymous, *The Housekeeper's Guide to Preserved Meats, Fruits, Vegetables, &c.* (London: Crosse & Blackwell, 1890), 144.

20. Cowen, *Relish*, 156.

21. Ibid.

22. Ibid., 243.

23. *The Musical World, XXXI* (London: Meyers & Co., 1853), 360.

24. Perhaps, despite his celebrity and triumphs, he still had something to prove—that he could outdo his hometown's best?

25. Nineteenth-century Crosse & Blackwell newspaper ad.

26. Ironically, Crosse & Blackwell's facilities were right on the edge of the vicinity of a famous cholera epidemic. In 1854, Dr. John Snow traced the source of the disease to a water pump on Broad Street, only a few blocks from the firm's Soho shop. Also, in July 1850, public concern about unsavory food additives led to the creation of the Public Health Act. As a result, Blackwell had to confess before Parliament that the firm had added poisonous copper sulfate and iron sulfate as food colorings to some of its products.

27. Soyer, *Modern Housewife*, 64.

CHAPTER 4. THE FRENCH WERE NOT, OF COURSE, THE ONLY SAUCIERS

1. A recipe is included in chapter 8, "Suspensions."

2. *Kanz al-Fawa'id fi tanwi' al-Mawa'id*, quoted in Lilia Zaouali, *Medieval Cuisine of the Arabic World: A Concise History with 174 Recipes*, trans. M. B. De-Bevoise, California Studies in Food and Culture (Berkeley: University of California Press, 2007), 65.

3. Warfare in the Middle East, especially in Syria, has made the growth and distribution of true Aleppo pepper almost impossible.

4. Gary Allen, *The Herbalist in the Kitchen* (Urbana: University of Illinois Press, 2007), 236–37.

5. Mothbeans, *Vigna aconitifolia*.

6. Asafoedita, the dried and powdered resin of *Ferula assafoetida*, a foul-smelling substance that, once cooked, adds a pleasant garlicky taste to foods.

7. A common but variable Indian spice blend that consists of a combination of different spices, among them black pepper, cardamom, coriander seed, cinnamon, cloves, cumin, powdered ginger, mace, and nutmeg, all ground together.

8. Black salt, a peculiarly sulfurous mineral collected in Bangladesh, northern India, Nepal, and Pakistan.

9. Sugar often made from the sap of date palms; brown sugar often serves as a substitute.

10. Discussed at length in chapter 7, "Solutions," and chapter 8, "Suspensions."

11. In sub-Saharan Africa, the ground seeds of various melons are added to soups and stews to thicken them in the same manner as nuts or pumpkin seeds. The dishes are collectively known as *egusi* or *agushi*.

CHAPTER 5. THE MODERN WORLD OF COOKING BEGINS

1. Auguste Escoffier, *Escoffier, Memories of My Life* (New York: Van Nostrand Reinhold, 1997), 119.

2. Priscilla Parkhurst Ferguson, *Accounting for Taste: The Triumph of French Cuisine* (Chicago: University of Chicago Press, 2004), 157.

3. Auguste Escoffier, *Escoffier Cookbook: A Guide to the Fine Art of French Cuisine* (New York: Crown, 1969), 20.

4. "Bechamel 101," *Escoffier*, http://courses.escoffieronline.com/bechamel-101.

5. "Veloute 101," *Escoffier*, http://courses.escoffieronline.com/veloute-101.

6. Escoffier, *Escoffier Cookbook*, 20.

7. "How to Make Sauce Espagnole," *Escoffier*, http://www.escoffieronline .com/how-to-make-sauce-espagnole.

8. Escoffier, *Escoffier Cookbook*, 18–20.

9. "How to Make Hollandaise Sauce," *Escoffier*, http://www.escoffieronline .com/how-to-make-hollandaise-sauce.

10. "Tomato Sauce," *BBC*, http://www.bbc.co.uk/food/recipes/tomatosauce _3755.

11. Escoffier, *Escoffier*, 180.

12. Quoted in ibid., xvi.

CHAPTER 6. TIME FOR A CHANGE

1. Mrs. Isabella Mary Beeton, *The Book of Household Management* (London: S. O. Beeton, 1861).

2. Auguste Escoffier, *Escoffier Cookbook: A Guide to the Fine Art of French Cuisine* (New York: Crown, 1969), 51.

3. "Ethnic" has come to be seen as a pejorative when applied to cuisines. It reeks of racist inferences to "the other" and is usually combined with an unwillingness to pay the higher prices deserved by other traditional—respectable (read: "European")—restaurants.

CHAPTER 7. SOLUTIONS

1. Brownian motion—heat, after all, is just movement; the faster the motion of the molecules, the higher the temperature.

2. This is an example of the many medieval recipes that members of the Society for Creative Anachronism have researched and re-created.

3. *Stephan's Florilegium* (http://www.florilegium.org).

4. The juice of wine grapes that has not yet fermented.

5. Escoffier, *Escoffier Cookbook*, 1.

6. A thick-leaved kelp, various species of *Saccharina* or *Laminaria*.

7. Perfumers often capture the airborne scent molecules of flowers on butter, where they stick to the butter's surface; they then extract those essences by washing them out with alcohol.

8. "Alici" hearkens back to Roman *allec*, the solid residue of decomposed fish left over when making *liquamen*. It's similar to the *pissalat* of today's Provence (which is anchovy paste flavored with bay leaf, black pepper, cloves, and thyme, thinned with a little olive oil).

9. Gary Allen, *Can It! The Perils and Pleasures of Preserving Food* (London: Reaktion, 2016), 203.

10. Chinese mixed ground, sweet spices: cinnamon, cloves, fennel seed, star anise, and szechuan peppercorns.

11. Emily Hahn, *The Cooking of China* (New York: Time-Life Books, 1968), 43.

12. The anthocyanin pigments in the cabbage are very pH sensitive. If cooked with alkaline baking soda instead of vinegar, the vegetable acquires a very unappetizing blue color.

13. The liquid is not, as commonly assumed, blood. All blood is carefully drained from meat during the slaughtering process.

14. Ian Chillag, "Sandwich Monday: Gravy Bread," *The Salt*, July 22, 2013, https://www.npr.org/sections/thesalt/2013/07/22/204535779/sandwich-monday -gravy-bread.

CHAPTER 8. SUSPENSIONS

1. The term "coulis" originally just meant "sauce" and referred specifically to meat juices, especially veal stock. It has gradually evolved to mean all kinds of purées of meats or vegetables. See Prosper Montagné, Nina Froud, and Charlotte Snyder Turgeon, *Larousse Gastronomique: The Encyclopedia of Food, Wine and Cookery* (London: Hamlyn, 1961), 310.

2. The company name comes from the Taiwanese freighter (with a Panamanian registry) on which sauce inventor David Tran emigrated from Vietnam to California.

3. Tran's current factory (650,000 square feet, in Irwindale, California) has drawn a lot of complaints from—and civil actions by—neighbors who don't appreciate the pungent aromas generated by the plant.

4. Bartolomeo Scappi and Terence Scully, *The Opera of Bartolomeo Scappi (1570)* (Toronto: University of Toronto Press, 2008), n.p.

5. Thomas Farrell, "A Tinned History of Crosse & Blackwell (1706–1914)," *Let's Look Again*, http://letslookagain.com/2014/10/crosse-blackwell.

6. Mrs. Isabella Mary Beeton, *The Book of Household Management* (London: S. O. Beeton, 1861), 715–16.

7. Karen Hess, *Martha Washington's Booke of Cookery: And Booke of Sweetmeats: Being a Family Manuscript, Curiously Copied by an Unknown Hand Sometime in the Seventeenth Century, Which Was in Her Keeping from 1749, the Time of Her Marriage to Daniel Custis, to 1799, at Which Time She Gave It to Eleanor Parke Custis, Her Granddaughter, on the Occasion of Her Marriage to Lawrence Lewis* (New York: Columbia University Press, 1981), 174.

8. Mary Randolph, *The Virginia Housewife or, Methodical Cook* (New York: Dover, 1993), 94–95.

9. Thomas P. Branston, *The Handbook of Practical Receipts, of Everyday Use* (Philadelphia: Lindsay & Blakiston, 1857), 148.

10. Ben Robinson, "Please Stop Trying to Serve Me House-Made Artisanal Organic Ketchup," *Thrillist*, September 23, 2015, https://www.thrillist.com/eat/nation/why-fancy-ketchup-is-stupid.

11. Joan Santanach, ed., *The Book of Sent Soví: Medieval Recipes from Catalonia*, trans. Robin Vogelzang (Barcelona: Barcino-Tamesis, 2014), 81.

12. The patent has long expired, and powdered mustard of the Colman variety is manufactured everywhere, under many brand names.

13. Quoted in Jacqueline Raposos, "Tim Graham's Secret Weapon," *Tasting Table*, April 14, 2015, https://www.tastingtable.com/cook/national/kasundi-recipe-homemade-condiment-tim-graham-chicago.

14. In the West, we think of coriander seeds as a spice and coriander leaves as the herb cilantro. In Thailand, all parts of the plant—leaves, roots, seeds, and stems—are thought of as separate ingredients and have different names.

15. These were formerly called "kaffir" limes, but the word is racially insensitive—it's an epithet used by whites to denigrate blacks in South Africa—so Thai *makrut* is preferred.

16. *Ped* equals "hot," *som* is "sour," *keo wan* means "green sweet," and *lueang* is simply "yellow" in Thai.

17. Gary Allen, *The Herbalist in the Kitchen* (Urbana: University of Illinois Press, 2007), 452.

18. A rotola was a Neapolitan measure of weight, roughly equal to two pounds. Quoted in Stefano Milioni, "The First Italian Tomato Recipes," *Italian Tribune*, March 27, 2014, http://www.italiantribune.com/the-first-italian-tomato-recipes.

19. Marinara doesn't exist as a separate sauce in Italy; in the United States, the word refers to any generic tomato sauce, especially in a jar. The name suggests that the sauce was a favorite of sailors.

20. The past participle of the verb *ragoûtier*, "to revive the taste."

21. Penelope Casas, *The Foods and Wines of Spain* (New York: Knopf, 2005), 214.

22. "U.S. Population: Which Brands of Whipped Topping (Cream Type) Do You Eat Most Often?," *Statista*, https://www.statista.com/statistics/278648/us-households-most-eaten-brands-of-whipped-topping-cream-type.

23. Anonymous, *A Proper Newe Booke of Cokerye* (London: Lant and Bankes, 1545; repr. 1560), 25.

24. The technique is really only a high-tech version of what we've been doing in barbecue pits for ages.

CHAPTER 9. GELS

1. Auguste Escoffier, *Escoffier Cookbook: A Guide to the Fine Art of French Cuisine* (New York: Crown, 1969), 17.

2. André Soltner, "André Soltner on Mother Sauces," *Lucky Peach*, May 27, 2015, http://luckypeach.com/andre-soltners-guide-to-mother-sauces.

3. Mammocks (known as cracklins in the United States) are crispy bits of pork left after the lard is rendered. Modern cooks, who purchase pure-white, already rendered lard, will not encounter any mammocks.

4. Quoted in Jonell Galloway, "What to Eat in France: The History of Sauce," *Rambling Epicure*, http://www.theramblingepicure.com/what-to-eat-in-france-the-history-of-sauce.

5. Eliza Leslie, *Miss Leslie's New Cookery Book* (Philadelphia: T. B. Peterson, 1857), 294.

6. The King had some unusual and distinctly nonroyal food preferences. His favorite sandwich is said to have been fried bacon (a full pound), with peanut butter and grape jelly, on Italian bread.

7. In some parts of Texas, the liquid part of chili con carne is "tightened" with a little masa harina.

8. Lye reacts with surface starch to give pretzels their gloss.

9. Harold McGee, *On Food and Cooking: The Science and Lore of the Kitchen,* 1st Scribner rev. ed. (New York: Scribner, 2004), 624.

CHAPTER 10. EMULSIONS

1. Actually, the cream doesn't rise; gravity pulls the heavier whey to the bottom.

2. Fannie Merritt Farmer, *The Original Boston Cooking-School Cookbook 1896* (facsimile) (New York: Weathervane Books, 1973), 290–91.

3. Edward Bottone, "Blended Me with Science!" *Table Matters,* June 7, 2016, http://tablematters.com/2016/06/07/blended-me-with-science.

4. In the Netherlands, mayonnaise must contain a minimum of 70 percent oil and 5 percent egg yolks. Like Miracle Whip, the much lighter Dutch *fritessaus*—which, as the name suggests, is a topping for fries—has only a fraction of mayonnaise's oil.

5. "Kraft Miracle Whip Consumer Insights," *InfoScout,* https://infoscout.co /brand/kraft_miracle_whip.

6. "Kraft Mayo Consumer Insights," *InfoScout,* https://infoscout.co/brand /kraft_mayo.

7. Finely chopped tomato that has first been seeded and peeled.

8. John Evelyn, *Acetaria: A Discourse of Sallets* (London, 1699), 14–15.

9. Greg Morabito, "Guy Fieri Admits That Donkey Sauce Is Just Aioli," *Eater,* https://www.eater.com/2017/6/27/15879670/guy-fieri-aioli-donkey-sauce.

10. Quoted in Maestra Suzanne de la Ferté, "Food and Feasting in Renaissance Italy," *Kingdom of Northchiefs,* September 2015, http://northshield.org/resources /pdf/moas/FoodFeastItalianRen.pdf, 10.

11. Harold McGee, *On Food and Cooking: The Science and Lore of the Kitchen,* 1st Scribner rev. ed. (New York: Scribner, 2004), 624.

CHAPTER 11. CULTURED SAUCES

1. Vegetarians and people who stick close to a Kosher diet avoid cheeses made with rennet. Various sour-plant-based compounds (nettle juice, for example) can accomplish very similar levels of protein denaturing.

2. Romanian *smântână* looks the same and sounds similar—it's just as thick as sour cream—but it is unfermented and sweet. It is not a substitute for the others listed here.

3. *Oxygala,* literally "sour milk." Owen Powell (trans.), *Galen: On the Properties of Foodstuffs* (Cambridge: Cambridge University Press, 2003), 127.

CHAPTER 12. COMPOSITES

1. Auguste Escoffier, *Escoffier Cookbook: A Guide to the Fine Art of French Cuisine* (New York: Crown, 1969), 42–43.

2. Hundreds of variations of *sauce américaine* exist. This is merely the simplest. Escoffier's, for example, is the by-product of an elaborate preparation of lobster, not a separate sauce.

3. Does that make *sauce choron* and *sauce valois* granddaughter sauces?

4. Mrs. W. G. Waters, *The Cook's Decameron: A Study in Taste* (London: W. Heinemann, 1901).

5. Escoffier, *Escoffier Cookbook*, 31.

6. Charles Elmé Francatelli, *The Modern Cook: A Practical Guide to the Culinary Art in All Its Branches, Adapted as Well for the Largest Establishments, as for the Use of Private Families* (London: Richard Bentley, 1846), 9–10.

7. Harold McGee, *On Food and Cooking: The Science and Lore of the Kitchen*, 1st Scribner rev. ed. (New York: Scribner, 2004), 596.

8. Some recipes add sugar, which somehow seems wrong. However, *sauce lagon bleu*, a Polynesian specialty, incorporates honey and chopped pickles in the basic Thousand Island formula, so who's to say?

9. Raymond A. Sokolov, *The Saucier's Apprentice: A Modern Guide to Classic French Sauces for the Home* (New York: Knopf, 1982), 106–7.

10. Samantha Schmidt, "Heinz Promotes Its New 'Mayochup' and Sparks an International Controversy," *Washington Post*, April 13, 2018.

11. McDonald's periodically offers special sandwiches topped with ketchup and Arch Sauce—a mixture of mayonnaise and brown mustard.

12. Many restaurant-goers perceive thick mayonnaise- and sour cream–based salad dressings as being less healthy than lighter vinaigrettes. This perception has not, however, stopped them from ordering blue cheese dressings.

13. Which, ironically, is descended from Southeast Asian sauces—lending some credence to the old "what goes around, comes around" maxim.

14. "Philippines Sauces," *Asian Recipes*, https://www.asian-recipe.com/philippines/philippines-sauces.html#sour_dipping_sauce.

15. This is not the same as Café de Paris butter, described elsewhere.

16. "Chinese Brown Sauce, Base Sauce, Mother Sauce or Kung Po Sauce," *Art of Cooking*, http://www.theartofcooking.org/chinese-american-recipes/chinese-brown-sauce-base-sauce-mother-sauce-or-kung-po-sauce.

17. Will Sellick, *The Imperial African Cookery Book* (London: Jeppestown Press, 2010), 214.

18. Eliza Leslie, *Directions for Cookery, in Its Various Branches: Forty-Ninth Edition, Thoroughly Revised with Additions* (Philadelphia: H. C. Baird, 1853), n.p.

19. Ibid.

20. "Austin Jewish Community BBQ Sauce," *Food Dictator*, December 30, 2014, https://www.thefooddictator.com/austin-jewish-community-bbq-sauce.

21. Maggi sauce gets its umami from hydrolyzed soy protein, yeast extract, and sodium glutamate, and it is slightly tangy due to citric and acetic acids.

22. It's interesting that ketchup, the quintessential Western condiment—which originated in southeastern Asia under Chinese influence—has found its way back into Chinese cuisine, at least in the kind of Chinese cooking that is common in the West.

AFTERWORD

1. Quoted in Nora Ephron, "Critics in the World of the Rising Soufflé (or Is It Meringue?)," *New York Magazine*, September 30, 1968.

2. Athenaeus, *The Deipnosophistae*, trans. Charles Burton Gulick (Cambridge, MA: Harvard University Press, 1927–1941), 9:169.

REFERENCES

Allen, Gary. *Can It! The Perils and Pleasures of Preserving Food*. London: Reaktion, 2016.

———. *The Herbalist in the Kitchen*. Urbana: University of Illinois Press, 2007.

Anonymous. *The Housekeeper's Guide to Preserved Meats, Fruits, Vegetables, &c.* London: Crosse & Blackwell, 1890.

———. *A Proper Newe Booke of Cokerye*. London: Lant and Bankes, 1545; repr. 1560. https://archive.org/stream/b21530191/b21530191_djvu.txt.

Anthimus. *Anthimus, De observatione ciborum: On the Observance of Foods*. Edited and translated by Mark Grant. Blackawton, Totnes, Devon, UK: Prospect Books, 1996.

Athenaeus. *The Deipnosophistae*. Translated by Charles Burton Gulick. Cambridge, MA: Harvard University Press, 1927–1941. http://penelope.uchicago.edu/Thayer/E/Roman/Texts/Athenaeus.

"Austin Jewish Community BBQ Sauce." *Food Dictator*. December 30, 2014. https://www.thefooddictator.com/austin-jewish-community-bbq-sauce.

"Bechamel 101." *Escoffier*. http://courses.escoffieronline.com/bechamel-101.

Beeton, Mrs. Isabella Mary. *The Book of Household Management*. London: S. O. Beeton, 1861.

Bottéro, Jean. *The Oldest Cuisine in the World: Cooking in Mesopotamia*. Chicago: University of Chicago Press, 2004.

Bottone, Edward. "Blended Me with Science!" *Table Matters*. June 7, 2016. http://tablematters.com/2016/06/07/blended-me-with-science.

Branston, Thomas P. *The Handbook of Practical Receipts, of Everyday Use*. Philadelphia: Lindsay & Blakiston, 1857.

Brillat-Savarin, Jean Anthelme. *The Physiology of Taste*. Translated by M. F. K. Fisher. New York: Limited Editions Club, 1949.

Bull, Marian. "The Mother Sauces of Spain." *Lucky Peach*. December 3, 2015. http://luckypeach.com/the-mother-sauces-of-spain.

Casas, Penelope. *The Foods and Wines of Spain*. New York: Knopf, 2005.

Chillag, Ian. "Sandwich Monday: Gravy Bread." *The Salt*. July 22, 2013. https://www.npr.org/sections/thesalt/2013/07/22/204535779/sandwich-monday-gravy-bread.

"Chinese Brown Sauce, Base Sauce, Mother Sauce or Kung Po Sauce." *Art of Cooking*. http://www.theartofcooking.org/chinese-american-recipes/chinese-brown-sauce-base-sauce-mother-sauce-or-kung-po-sauce.

Cowen, Ruth. *Relish: The Extraordinary Life of Alexis Soyer, Victorian Celebrity Chef*. London: Orion Books, 2007.

Dalby, Andrew. *Siren Feasts: A History of Food and Gastronomy in Greece*. London: Routledge, 1996.

de la Ferté, Maestra Suzanne. "Food and Feasting in Renaissance Italy." *Kingdom of Northchiefs*. September 2015. http://northshield.org/resources/pdf/moas/FoodFeastItalianRen.pdf.

de Worde, Wynkyn. *The Boke of Keruynge*. East Sussex, UK: Southover Press, 2003.

Dumas, Alexandre. *Dumas on Food*. Translated by Alan and Jane Davidson. London: Folio Society, 1978.

Ephron, Nora. "Critics in the World of the Rising Souffle (or Is It Meringue?)." *New York Magazine*. September 30, 1968.

Escoffier, Auguste. *Escoffier Cookbook: A Guide to the Fine Art of French Cuisine*. New York: Crown, 1969.

———. *Escoffier, Memories of My Life*. New York: Van Nostrand Reinhold, 1997.

Evelyn, John. *Acetaria: A Discourse of Sallets*. London, 1699.

Farmer, Fannie Merritt. *The Original Boston Cooking-School Cookbook 1896* (facsimile). New York: Weathervane Books, 1973.

Farrell, Thomas. "A Tinned History of Crosse & Blackwell (1706–1914)." *Let's Look Again*. http://letslookagain.com/2014/10/crosse-blackwell.

Ferguson, Priscilla Parkhurst. *Accounting for Taste: The Triumph of French Cuisine*. Chicago: University of Chicago Press, 2004.

Fettiplace, Elinor, and Hilary Spurling. *Elinor Fettiplace's Receipt Book: Elizabethan Country House Cooking*. London: Viking Salamander, 1986.

Francatelli, Charles Elmé. *The Modern Cook: A Practical Guide to the Culinary Art in All Its Branches, Adapted as Well for the Largest Establishments, as for the Use of Private Families*. London: Richard Bentley, 1846.

Galloway, Jonell. "What to Eat in France: The History of Sauce." *Rambling Epi-cure.* http://www.theramblingepicure.com/what-to-eat-in-france-the-history-of -sauce.

Glasse, Hannah. *The Art of Cookery Made Plain and Easy; Which Far Exceeds Any Thing of the Kind Yet Published.* London, 1774.

Grocock, Christopher, and Sally Grainger. *Apicius: A Critical Edition with an Introduction and an English Translation of the Latin Recipe Text.* Totnes, UK: Prospect, 2006.

Hahn, Emily. *The Cooking of China.* New York: Time-Life Books, 1968.

Hess, Karen. *Martha Washington's Booke of Cookery: And Booke of Sweetmeats: Be-ing a Family Manuscript, Curiously Copied by an Unknown Hand Sometime in the Seventeenth Century, Which Was in Her Keeping from 1749, the Time of Her Marriage to Daniel Custis, to 1799, at Which Time She Gave It to Eleanor Parke Custis, Her Granddaughter, on the Occasion of Her Marriage to Lawrence Lewis.* New York: Columbia University Press, 1981.

"How to Make Hollandaise Sauce." *Escoffier.* http://www.escoffieronline.com /how-to-make-hollandaise-sauce.

"How to Make Sauce Espagnole." *Escoffier.* http://www.escoffieronline.com/how -to-make-sauce-espagnole.

"How We Make Original Red Sauce." *Tabasco.* http://www.tabasco.com/tabasco -products/how-its-made/making-original-tabasco-sauce.

Jaucourt, Louis, chevalier de. "Sauce." *The Encyclopedia of Diderot & d'Alembert Collaborative Translation Project.* Translated by Sean Takats. http://hdl.handle .net/2027/spo.did2222.0000.666.

Jenkins, Tom. "The Basque Mother Sauces Explained." *Fine Dining Lovers.* Au-gust 3, 2017. https://www.finedininglovers.com/stories/basque-mother-sauces.

Juvenal. *The Satires of Juvenal.* Translated by Rolfe Humphries. Bloomington: Indiana University Press, 1958.

Kelley, Laura. "New Flavors for the Oldest Recipes." *Aramco World.* November/ December 2012. http://archive.aramcoworld.com/issue/201206/new.flavors.for .the.oldest.recipes.htm.

Kelly, Ian. *Cooking for Kings: The Life of Antonin Carême, the First Celebrity Chef.* New York: Walker, 2004.

"Kraft Mayo Consumer Insights." *InfoScout.* https://infoscout.co/brand/kraft _mayo.

"Kraft Miracle Whip Consumer Insights." *InfoScout.* https://infoscout.co/brand /kraft_miracle_whip.

Leslie, Eliza. *Directions for Cookery, in Its Various Branches: Forty-Ninth Edition, Thoroughly Revised with Additions.* Philadelphia: H. C. Baird, 1853.

———. *Miss Leslie's New Cookery Book*. Philadelphia: T. B. Peterson, 1857.

Martinelli, C., trans. *Anonymous Andalusian Cookbook from the 13th Century. Candida Martinelli's Italophile Site*. http://italophiles.com/andalusian_cookbook.pdf.

McGee, Harold. *On Food and Cooking: The Science and Lore of the Kitchen*. 1st Scribner rev. ed. New York: Scribner, 2004.

Memoirs of Alexis Soyer: With Unpublished Receipts and Odds and Ends of Gastronomy. Edited by F. Volant and J. R. Warren. Cambridge: Cambridge University Press, 2013.

Milioni, Stefano. "The First Italian Tomato Recipes." *Italian Tribune*. March 27, 2014. http://www.italiantribune.com/the-first-italian-tomato-recipes.

Montagné, Prosper, Nina Froud, and Charlotte Snyder Turgeon. *Larousse Gastronomique: The Encyclopedia of Food, Wine and Cookery*. London: Hamlyn, 1961.

Montaigne, Michel de. *The Essays of Michel de Montaigne*. Translated by George B. Ives. New York: Heritage Press, 1946.

Morabito, Greg. "Guy Fieri Admits That Donkey Sauce Is Just Aioli." *Eater*. https://www.eater.com/2017/6/27/15879670/guy-fieri-aioli-donkey-sauce.

The Musical World, XXXI. London: Meyers & Co., 1853.

"The Original Tomato Sauce." *Vintage Cookbook Trials*. https://vintagecookbook trials.wordpress.com/2013/04/11/the-original-tomato-sauce.

"Our Guide to Escoffier's 5 Mother Sauces." *Escoffier*. http://www.escoffieronline .com/our-guide-to-escoffiers-5-mother-sauces.

Pegge, Samuel. *The Forme of Cury: A Roll of Ancient English Cookery Compiled, about A.D. 1390*. Project Gutenberg. http://www.gutenberg.org/ebooks/8102.

Peterson, James. *Sauces: Classical and Contemporary Sauce Making*. 2nd ed. New York: Van Nostrand Reinhold, 1998.

Peterson, T. Sarah. *Acquired Taste: The French Origins of Modern Cooking*. Ithaca, NY: Cornell University Press 1994.

Petronius. *The Satyricon*. Translated by William Arrowsmith. Ann Arbor: University of Michigan Press, 1959.

"Philippines Sauces." *Asian Recipes*. https://www.asian-recipe.com/philippines /philippines-sauces.html#sour_dipping_sauce.

Powell, Owen, trans. *Galen: On the Properties of Foodstuffs*. Cambridge: Cambridge University Press, 2003.

Power, Eileen, trans. *The Goodman of Paris (le Ménagier de Paris): A Treatise on Moral and Domestic Economy by a Citizen of Paris, c. 1393*. Woodbridge, UK: Boydell Press, 2006.

Randolph, Mary. *The Virginia Housewife or, Methodical Cook*. New York: Dover, 1993.

Raposos, Jacqueline. "Tim Graham's Secret Weapon." *Tasting Table*. April 14, 2015. https://www.tastingtable.com/cook/national/kasundi-recipe-homemade -condiment-tim-graham-chicago.

Redding, Ann. "The Mother Sauces of Thailand." *Lucky Peach*. May 22, 2015. http://luckypeach.com/the-mother-sauces-of-thailand.

Robinson, Ben. "Please Stop Trying to Serve Me House-Made Artisanal Organic Ketchup." *Thrillist*. September 23, 2015. https://www.thrillist.com/eat/nation /why-fancy-ketchup-is-stupid.

Rogers, Katharine M. *Pork: A Global History*. London: Reaktion Books, 2012.

Santanach, Joan, ed. *The Book of Sent Soví: Medieval Recipes from Catalonia*. Translated by Robin Vogelzang. Barcelona: Barcino-Tamesis, 2014.

Scappi, Bartolomeo, and Terence Scully. *The Opera of Bartolomeo Scappi (1570)*. Toronto: University of Toronto Press, 2008.

Schmidt, Samantha. "Heinz Promotes Its New 'Mayochup' and Sparks an International Controversy." *Washington Post*. April 13, 2018.

Sellick, Will. *The Imperial African Cookery Book*. London: Jeppestown Press, 2010.

Sokolov, Raymond A. *The Saucier's Apprentice: A Modern Guide to Classic French Sauces for the Home*. New York: Knopf, 1982.

Soltner, André. "André Soltner on Mother Sauces." *Lucky Peach*. May 27, 2015. http://luckypeach.com/andre-soltners-guide-to-mother-sauces.

Soyer, Alexis Benoist. *The Gastronomic Regenerator: A Simplified and Entirely New System of Cookery, with Nearly Two Thousand Practical Receipts Suited to the Income of All Classes*. 6th ed. London: Simpkin, Marshall, & Co., Stationers' Hall Court, 1849.

———. *The Modern Housewife*. New York: D. Appleton & Co., 1851.

Tebben, Maryann. *Sauces: A Global History*. London: Reaktion Books, 2014.

Tirel, Guillaume. *Le viandier de Taillevent*. Translated by James Prescott. http:// www.telusplanet.net/public/prescotj/data/viandier.

"Tomato Sauce." *BBC*. http://www.bbc.co.uk/food/recipes/tomatosauce_3755.

"U.S. Population: Which Brands of Whipped Topping (Cream Type) Do You Eat Most Often?" *Statista*. https://www.statista.com/statistics/278648/us-house holds-most-eaten-brands-of-whipped-topping-cream-type.

"Veloute 101." *Escoffier*. http://courses.escoffieronline.com/veloute-101.

Waters, Mrs. W. G. *The Cook's Decameron: A Study in Taste*. London: W. Heinemann, 1901.

Winters, Ruth. *A Consumer's Dictionary of Food Additives*. 4th ed. New York: Three Rivers Press, 1994.

Zaouali, Lilia. *Medieval Cuisine of the Arabic World: A Concise History with 174 Recipes.* Translated by M. B. DeBevoise. California Studies in Food and Culture. Berkeley: University of California Press, 2007.

Zhou Hongcheng. "Salt and Sauce in the Chinese Culinary." *Flavor & Fortune* 16 (Spring 2009): 9–10. http://www.flavorandfortune.com/dataaccess/article.php?ID=699.

INDEX